James George Maguire

Ireland and the Pope

A brief history of papal intrigues against Irish liberty from Adrian IV. to Leo XIII. Third Edition

James George Maguire

Ireland and the Pope
*A brief history of papal intrigues against Irish liberty from Adrian IV. to Leo XIII.
Third Edition*

ISBN/EAN: 9783337103057

Printed in Europe, USA, Canada, Australia, Japan

Cover: Foto ©ninafisch / pixelio.de

More available books at **www.hansebooks.com**

IRELAND AND THE POPE.

A BRIEF HISTORY

OF

PAPAL INTRIGUES

AGAINST IRISH LIBERTY

FROM

Adrian IV. to Leo XIII.

By JAMES G. MAGUIRE,

EX-JUDGE OF THE SUPERIOR COURT OF SAN FRANCISCO, CALIFORNIA.

THIRD EDITION.

SAN FRANCISCO:
JAMES H. BARRY, 429 MONTGOMERY STREET.
1890.

Ireland and The Pope.

A BRIEF HISTORY

OF

PAPAL INTRIGUES

Against Irish Liberty

FROM

Adrian IV. to Leo XIII.

By James G. Maguire,

JUDGE OF THE SUPERIOR COURT OF SAN FRANCISCO, CALIFORNIA.

> "*The Rescript must be obeyed.*"
> J. Cardinal Simeoni.

> "Aye,
> They can crush us as in ages flown.
> What to them is a nation's anguish?—
> Nothing more than a dying groan."
> Una.

SAN FRANCISCO:
JAMES H. BARRY, 429 MONTGOMERY STREET.
1888.

DEDICATION.

To the heroes who, in spite of popes and kings, poured their blood on the altar of Irish liberty, and thus kept alive the patriot flame, through the long centuries of Ireland's night of slavery; and to all the living priests and people who believe that Ireland's struggle for liberty should not be postponed to await the pleasure of any foreign potentate, this book is affectionately dedicated.

THE AUTHOR.

CONTENTS.

	PAGE.
Dedication	3
Preface	5
Chapter I—Introduction	9
II—Bull of Adrian IV	14
III—The Bull of Pope Alexander III. and the Synod of Cashel	20
IV—Humiliating the Irish Priests and People	26
V—Papal Interference with Irish Struggles for Liberty after the Conquest	38
VI—The Religious Wars	41
VII—A sop to Cerberus	45
VIII—The Repeal Movement killed by a Rescript	49
IX—The Young Ireland Movement killed by Bishops and Priests	57
X—The Fenian Movement Opposed by the Church	71
XI—The Home Rule Movement Opposed by the Church	73
XII—The Land League Opposed by the Pope	76
XIII—The Last Rescript	83
XIV—Plan of Campaign and Boycott vs. Rack Rent, Eviction and Rules of Estate	84
XV—Pope Leo's Boycott on Dr. McGlynn	96
XVI—Vatican Politics—the Italian Ring	100
XVII—Conclusion	110
List of Authorities	114
Appendix A—Full translation of the Bull of Pope Adrian IV. granting Ireland to King Henry II	115
Appendix B—Full translation of the Bull of Pope Alexander III. confirming the grant of Adrian	116
Appendix C—The text of the last Rescript	117

PREFACE.

This book is written to supply what I conceive to be not only a demand but a real necessity. Its purpose is to show the wrong and injustice of papal interference with the struggles of the Irish people to regain the national independence which they lost through the treachery of an English pope.

To show the extent, persistence and deadly character of that interference.

And to point out the necessity, and the patriotic duty of firmly and constantly rejecting and resisting every political edict, issued by a pope or inquisition, respecting Irish affairs.

I am painfully aware of the extreme difficulty, if not impossibility, of exposing and condemning the political errors and faults of one who is the spiritual head of a church, without working some injury to the church which he represents.

To the delicacy and difficulty of this position, I attribute the otherwise remarkable circumstance that the very interesting and important facts herein set forth have never before been presented in any collected or connected form.

But the occasion demands that those facts be now given to the world fully and fairly, without either malice or timidity. Whatever the reader may think of the conclusions, which I have freely and candidly stated, he will find the statements of fact to be reliable and can readily verify all the more important of them by referring to the authorities which I have fully cited.

I conceive it to be a most marvelous record of an alliance of centuries, which has been characterized by constant and simple faith and confidence, on one side, and equally constant duplicity, ingratitude and tyranny on the other.

To the ultramontanes who may read this book and whose stereotyped criticism I may now fairly anticipate, I have but to say, that it is not my fault that the spiritual heads of the Catholic Church claim also to be, by divine right, temporal rulers, theoretically, over all nations, and in terrible reality over Ireland.

It is not my fault, but more shame to them, if the publication of the political history which *they* have made, shall disadvantage the church whose spiritual interests were confided to them, and should have been their first and constant care.

On this subject I can only add that I am not in the business of proselyting and disclaim any such purpose.

I speak neither as a friend nor as an enemy of the Catholic religion, and have said not a word concerning its doctrines, its principles, its sacraments or its forms.

The truth, or falsity, the soundness or unsoundness of the articles and rules of faith of that religion have nothing to do with Ireland's right to independent nationality or to Home Rule.

I desire, above all things, to separate those two questions by a wide and unmistakable line, and to distinguish, as well as I may, between the dual —religious and political—capacities which the Pope, unfortunately, occupies.

I speak as an American descendant of the Irish race; as an admirer of the Irish character; as a sympathizer in the struggles and trials of the Irish people and in their hereditary aspirations for liberty.

That a man may be a good Catholic and at the same time an Irish patriot, seven centuries of so-called "sedition," in which the people were often led by their *soggarths aroon*, attest.

That a man may reject the tenets of the Catholic religion and yet be an equally good Irish patriot, bear witness: Grattan, Emmet, Wolfe Tone, Davis, Mitchel, Parnell, and all the brave leaders and soldiers of Protestant faith, who, for more than a century, have graced and glorified the political and military struggles for Irish liberty.

While I believe and declare that religion has and should have nothing to do with Irish politics, I have, in writing this book, a purpose which the public mind will not wholly disconnect from religion, principally because the art and finesse of religio-political Italian statesmanship have so interwoven questions of religion and politics.

That purpose is to assist in raising my father's

countrymen and my own kinsmen above that groveling fear of the Pope, which makes so many of them nerveless when he strikes a blow at their country and their race, and above their present discreditable confidence in men who have proved themselves "the veriest slaves of treachery."

There is no other people on earth that the Pope would treat as he is treating, or as he has treated, the Irish; and this is simply because there is no other people on earth—not even one of the half-Indian states of South America—that would tolerate such political interference at his hands.

The Pope, in this respect, enjoys the unenviable, not to say infamous, distinction of being *dangerous only to those who confide in him.* I confidently expect that my work will meet with the approval not only of Irish patriots, of all shades of religious belief, but that it will be acceptable to the thinking Catholics of every country, who cannot fail to realize how greatly the true interests of the Catholic Church would be advanced by relieving it of the incubus of political intrigue against which my blows are aimed.

JAMES G. MAGUIRE.

San Francisco, June 4th, 1888.

CHAPTER I.

INTRODUCTION.

"The Holy Father must have been misinformed by evil advisers, or he would never have taken sides with English tyranny and landlord robbery against our sorely oppressed and long suffering people," said a devout Catholic and brave but disheartened Irish patriot to me a few days since. "Do you think," I asked, "that Archbishop Walsh, who has been for some time in Rome consulting with the Pope on the Irish question, made false statements to the detriment of his people?" "Oh, no, indeed," he replied. "I refer to the Duke of Norfolk, Errington, Monsignor Persico and other anti-Irish aristocrats and Castle Catholics, who are, unfortunately, nearer to His Holiness than are the friends of Ireland."

This good man is but one among thousands, aye millions, who firmly believe that the Pope has been imposed upon by false information concerning the Irish question.

The absurdity of this theory must be at once apparent to all who stop to think that there are in Ireland about twenty-eight bishops and archbishops, and thousands of priests, all in the immediate service of, under the control of, and in direct communication with, the Vatican, and that this great and intelligent body of men are thoroughly conversant with the minutest details of the every-day life of the people of all parts of Ireland.

To say that he is ignorant of the true state of Irish affairs is to assume that he does not think the Irish priesthood worth consulting; and, to say that he has been deceived by a few English and pro-English intriguers, is to assume that he attaches more value to the statements of a few secret emissaries than he does to the solemn official testimony of this great body of pious and devoted bishops and priests.

No, the Pope is not misinformed concerning the Irish question. He has acted deliberately, upon full knowledge, and upon a resolution formed more than one year ago, and, like his sudden support of Bismarck, "the arch enemy and persecutor of the Catholic Church," this act had a political price, which it is to be hoped Lord Salisbury may never be able to pay.

But, you may ask: "What evidence have you to support the statement that the present papal blow at the Irish national movement was premeditated for more than a year?" To this question I answer by presenting the two principal and all-sufficient facts, namely:

1. Monsignor Persico, in his letter of October last to the Pope, expressly shows that he was sent to Ireland to pave the way for the destruction of the Irish National League.

2. The edict is in perfect harmony with the course of the Vatican concerning Irish political affairs for more than seven hundred years.

Monsignor Persico was not sent to Ireland "for the purpose of learning, by actual observation, the true condition and political methods of the Irish people," as the telegraph informed us at the time of his visit, but for the purpose of cajoling and coercing the Irish priesthood into leaving and opposing the Irish National League.

This purpose was disclosed by the publication at Rome of a letter sent by him to the Pope, in October last, in which he expressed regret that his mission thus far had been a failure, because "the Irish priests would not abandon the political struggle of their countrymen, even when urged to do so in the name of the Pontiff and for the good of the Church."

While this treacherous ecclesiastical statesman, " this genial confidante and general spy," who, ac-

cording to his own confession, was in Ireland as a
secret enemy of the Irish cause, doing the work of
"Bloody Balfour" and his Tory master, he was
winning loud applause from the Irish people by
praising "with mimic openness of soul," their devotion and submission to the Holy Father, and
assuring them of the latter's deep and unwavering
love.

It is said that when Cortez, with his little band
of freebooters, entered the populous and hospitable
districts of Mexico, *he* won his way largely by
teaching the divine truths of Christianity to the
people whom he had come to rob and outrage, to
enslave and murder.

I believe it was Lawrence Sterne who said:
"Of all the cants that were ever canted in this
world, the cant of hypocrisy is the worst."

But the whole history of Vatican interference
with Irish politics shows an unbroken line, for
seven hundred years, of acts hostile to the liberties and natural rights of the Irish people.

The subjugation of Ireland to English rule, as
is well known to all students of Irish history, was
not accomplished by the force of English arms,
but by the decree and grant of Pope Adrian IV.,[*]

---

[*] See full translation of bull, Appendix A.

supplemented and enforced by the decrees and orders of Pope Alexander III.*

While, as I have said, these facts are well known to all students of Irish history, and while they are fully attested by every Irish historian worthy of the name, clerical influences have always kept the great masses of the Irish people in ignorance of them, so that to-day not one among a hundred of the Irish people knows how their country lost her nationality, and still fewer are aware of the persistent efforts of the successors of Adrian and Alexander to keep Ireland in the slavery to which their infamous bargain delivered her.

I shall, therefore, commence with the beginning, and make a plain, brief statement of the facts in chronological order, giving specific reference to my authorities, so that those who have the leisure and desire may conveniently test the accuracy of my statements, or study the details of events and transactions of which I can here give but a general outline.

Finding the standard Irish and Catholic histories sufficiently full and accurate upon these questions for my purpose, I have rejected all others, save in the matter of Lord Palmerston's intrigues with the Vatican, the most satisfactory evidence of

---

* See full translation of bull, Appendix B.

which I find in his biography ; and in the matter of the later intrigues of Pius IX. and Leo XIII., which have not yet reached the pages of authentic Irish history, but which are fresh in the minds of all sympathizers with the cause against which they were aimed.

CHAPTER II.
BULL OF ADRIAN IV.

In the year 1152 Ireland was a prosperous and independent nation, holding "her place among the nations of the earth."

Then it was that: "Argosies, laden with riches the rarest, gracefully dipped their proud ensigns" to her banner.

Her people were Catholics, and had for many generations looked lovingly to the Pope of Rome as their spiritual father, but they neither owned nor recognized any political allegiance to him. Then, as now, the Irish people were noted for their bravery, chivalry and generosity; but, then, they were learned* and respected for that most priceless quality of respectability—political independence—whilst now, and, alas, through all the dark and cruel centuries that have intervened, they have been crushed in ignorance, humiliation and

---

* Pope Adrian himself was "instructed in philosophy and divinity by Marianus O'Gorman, an Irish professor." O'Halloran's Hist., Bk. XIII, Ch. III, p. 307.

dependence between the upper and the nether millstone of Italian intrigue and British tyranny.

In that fatal year Cardinal John Paparo appeared in Ireland* as the special legate of Pope Eugenius III. He was the first Italian legate ever sent to Ireland—may Persico be the last! He summoned the bishops and principal priests to the Synod of Kells, and there delivered palliums† to the archbishops, taking their oaths of obedience to the Pope.

From that hour dates the downfall of Irish nationality. The spirit of Clontarf never ceased to animate them, but from that hour the children of Erin, though foremost and bravest in the armies of liberty throughout the world, have been slaves at home The people who had overwhelmed the powerful Danes and driven them from their shores, tamely bowed their heads to receive the yoke of the Saxons. Why? We need

---

* Haverty's Hist. Ireland, Chap. XVI., p. 162.

† The pallium is "a band of white wool, worn on the shoulders. It has two strings of the same material and four purple crosses worked on it. It is worn by the Pope and sent by him to patriarchs, primates, archbishops, and sometimes, though rarely, to bishops, as a token that they possess the 'fullness of the episcopal office'. Two lambs are brought annually to the church of St. Agnes at Rome, by the Apostolic sub-deacons, while the 'Agnus Dei' is being sung. These lambs are presented at the altar and received by two canons of the Lateran Church. From this wool the pallia are made by the nuns of Torre de Specchi. The sub-deacons lay the pallia on the tomb of St. Peter, where they remain all night."

Catholic Dictionary, Addis & Arnold, Tit. "Pallium."

not seek far for the answer. With the coming of Cardinal Paparo, his palliums and his oaths of obedience, came also the claim of temporal sovereignty asserted by the Pope.

This temporal power was speedily turned to the Pope's financial and political advantage. In the year 1154 Henry II. became King of England, and shortly afterwards sent John of Salisbury to Rome as a Royal emissary.* The King desired to add Ireland to his kingdom, and the Pope desired to put Ireland under tribute to the Vatican ; the Irish people having previously "paid those small dues called Peter's pence to the See of Armagh, which the rest of Europe paid to Rome."†

In the year 1156 Pope Adrian IV. gave to Henry II., King of England, a bull granting to him the political sovereignty of Ireland; addressing him as " my dearest son in Christ, the illustrious King of England;" authorizing him " to enter Ireland, to reduce the people to obedience under the laws, and to extirpate the plants of vice," on condition that he would " pay from each (meaning from each Irish family) a yearly pension of one penny to St. Peter, and that you will preserve the rights of the churches of this land inviolate."‡

---

* Haverty's Hist., Chap. XVIII., p. 188.
† O'Halloran's Hist. Ireland, Bk. XII., Chap. VI., p. 285.
‡ This bull, copies of which are in the ancient Vatican records, is pub-

The genuineness of this bull is attested by all of the Irish historians, except Abbe MacGeoghegan* and Thomas Mooney, from Geraldus Cambrensis in 1178, to the Nun of Kenmare in 1876, and the last edition of Haverty by Thomas Kelly in 1885.†

The Nun of Kenmare says of this bull: "There can be no reasonable doubt of the authenticity of this document. Baronius publsihed it from the *Codex Vaticanus*; John XXII. (Pope), annexed it to his brief addressed to Edward II. (Edward III.); and John of Salisbury (Catholic Bishop of Chartres, then secretary to the Arch- of Canterbury, states distinctly in his *Metalogicus*, that *he obtained this bull* from Adrian."‡

To the same effect, citing further proofs, is Haverty,|| while Dr. O'Halloran ("The Irish

---
lished in full, in the original Latin text, by Dr. O'Halloran (Hist. p. 310), and full translations are published by O'Halloran (Hist. p. 305); Haverty (Hist. p. 189); Wright (Hist. Ireland, p. 85); Ferguson (The Irish Before the Conquest, p. 288); and Walsh (Irish Hierarchy, p. 662.) See Appendix A.

* In his history of Ireland, as translated by Dr. Kelly (p. 18), the Abbe states that the bull was procured from Adrian, but he subsequently makes an argument to discredit its genuineness.

† O'Halloran's Hist., pp. 305 to 311; Haverty's Hist., pp. 187 to 193; McGee's Hist. Ireland, Vol. I, p. 136; Carew's Ecclesiastical Hist. Ireland, pp 282-3-6; Cusack (Nun of Kenmare) Hist. Ireland, pp. 274-5; McCarthy's Outlines of Irish Hist., p. 24; O'Callaghan's Notes and Illustrations in "Macariae Excidium"; Wright's Hist. Ireland, p. 85; Walsh's Irish Hierarchy, pp. 661-2.

‡ Hist., p. 275, note.

Hist., p. 190 and note.

Livy") and Dr. O'Callaghan very conclusively prove its genuineness.

St. Lawrence O'Toole and other leading bishops of Ireland conversed with Pope Alexander III. about this bull, and his own confirmatory bull, at the third general council of Lateran in 1179, and the Pope "became at length convinced that *in the confirmatory brief which he had drawn up for Henry*, he had been grossly deceived, and that the terms that were employed in that official document were as severe as they had been unmerited and uncalled for."* He was justly indignant, but *he did not recall the bull*.

Gerald de Barri (Geraldus Cambrensis,) a leading Catholic prelate of the time of Popes Adrian and Alexander, noted for having preached the principal sermon before the Synod of Dublin in 1177, published in the year 1178, during the lifetime of Alexander, a history of Ireland in which he inserted, in full, the bulls of both Adrian and Alexander in the Latin text, and their genuineness was not challenged.†

In addition to the frail denials of MacGeoghegan and Mooney, following him, I have before me a very ingenious but radically defective essay by

---
* Walsh's Irish Hierarchy, pp. 663-4.
† O'Halloran Hist., Bk. XIII., Chap. III., pp. 306-7.

Bishop Moran of Ossory,* written to prove that the alleged bull of Adrian was "a great Norman forgery." He discredits the statement of Cardinal Baronius, made three hundred years ago, that he had copied the bull of Adrian from the "Vatican Manuscript," because he (Moran) could not find the same manuscript three hundred years later.

He also discredits the *Bullarium Romanum* (a collection of papal bulls made under the authority of the Holy See), printed over one hundred and fifty years ago.

He also discredits the statement of John of Salisbury, Bishop of Chartres, made and published over seven hundred years ago, that he (John) had personally received the bull from Adrian and delivered it to Henry II.

Verily, "faith *will* move mountains" of historical evidence. There are other very conclusive proofs of its genuineness, to which he does not refer at all.

Father Burke's statement that this bull was a forgery is based entirely on this essay of Dr. Moran, and may be dismissed with it.†

---
* Irish Am. Library, "English Misrule in Ireland," p. 224.
† English Misrule in Ireland, pp. 27-8.

CHAPTER III.

THE BULL OF POPE ALEXANDER III. AND THE SYNOD OF CASHEL.

Henry II., for various reasons connected with the vicissitudes of England, did not make any use, now known to us, of the Bull of Adrian for fifteen years after receiving it. Adrian being then dead, Henry applied to Pope Alexander III. for a confirmation of the grant of Ireland. In the year 1172 Pope Alexander issued a bull addressed to his "most dear son in Christ, the illustrious King of England," and commencing thus: "Forasmuch as these things which have been, on good reasons, granted by our predecessors, deserve to be confirmed in the fullest manner; and considering the grant of the Dominion of Ireland by the venerable Pope Adrian, we, pursuing his footsteps, do ratify and confirm the same, reserving to St. Peter and to the Holy Roman Church, as well in England as in Ireland, the yearly pension of one penny from every house."*

That everlasting yearly "penny from every house" again—the price of poor Ireland's liberty!

---
* O'Halloran's Hist., p. 306; Wright's Hist., p. 86; Haverty's Hist., p. 191.

It has been faithfully paid. England's promise to the Vatican has been faithfully fulfilled to the letter; but alas, every penny of the tribute has been stained with the blood and tears of Erin's subjugated children.

Armed with these bulls, King Henry, who, before receiving the last, had entered Ireland (October 18th, 1171), claiming it under that of Adrian IV., immediately summoned the principal clergy of Ireland to meet in conference at Cashel.

This conference is historically known as the "Synod of Cashel." Here the Bulls of Adrian and Alexander were read, and, "in the name of the Sovereign Pontiff, the clergy and people of Ireland were called upon to receive Henry the Second of England as their king."*

At this Synod the Pope's Legate presided, St. Gelasius, the Primate of Ireland, having refused to attend.†

Mooney (who attempts to prove the bulls forgeries, to shield, as far as possible, the honor of the Vatican) says that they were read at this Synod, and thus graphically describes their effect: "Each man looked at his neighbor, not knowing what decision to make. The ecclesiastics were

---

* O'Halloran's Hist., p. 305; Mooney's Hist., p. 561, et seq.

† O'Halloran's Hist., pp. 310 and 313; Walsh's Irish Hierarchy, p. 195. et seq.

seized with panic and indecision. Some of the clergy inclined to the admonitions of the Pope and submitted to Henry, whilst others went their ways to their respective provinces, as much in grief as in anger. Some of the secondary chiefs of the south gave up their territories to Henry, receiving the same back to hold as his vassals; and, as this act of submission appeared not humiliating, owing to the acquiescence of so many of the clergy in the ordinance of the See of Rome, *Henry obtained the adherence of seven counties without striking a blow.*"*

Martin Haverty, while admitting the genuineness of the bulls, also attempts to shield the Popes, by claiming that the bulls had very little to do with the submission of the Irish people to the rule of England. This is contrary to the proofs of all contemporaneous history, and is simply absurd.† Five hundred and seventy-three years ago, when the details of her subjugation were fresh in the public and private annals of Ireland, and in the full traditions of her sorrowing people, Donnell O'Neill, King of Ulster, wrote his celebrated, learned, and statesmanlike letter to Pope John XXII., protesting against the great injustice done to Ireland by the Vatican, and declaring that

---

* Mooney's Hist., p. 561.
† Hist., p. 189.

Ireland was subjugated solely by the bull of Adrian.

Here is a striking passage from his letter.

"During the course of so many ages (three thousand years) our sovereigns preserved the independency of their country; attacked more than once by foreign powers, they wanted neither force nor courage to repel the bold invaders: *but that which they dared to do against force, they could not do against the simple decree of one of your predecessors—Adrian.*"*

Whether the bulls of Adrian and Alexander were forged or genuine is a matter of small consequence compared with the doubly established fact that the *claim* of temporal, kingly authority (as distinguished from religious authority) over Ireland by the popes, and the *acknowledgment* of that claim by the Irish people, caused the subjugation of Ireland to English rule. If that claim had not been acknowledged, the bulls, whether forged or genuine, would have been repudiated, and the armies of Henry would have been driven into the sea.†

But the genuineness of these bulls is overwhelmingly proved by historical evidence, and

---
* O'Halloran's Hist., p. 307; Mooney's Hist., p. 564; Haverty's Hist., p. 255.

† O'Halloran's Hist., p. 305; Mooney's Hist., pp. 560-2-4-8.

that which I have cited is, for the present, quite sufficient.

The contradictions among recognized Irish historians, concerning the reading of the bulls at the Synod of Cashel, results, probably, from the fact that no formal action was taken on them by the Synod as a body.

But that they were read and that there were individual submissions of the clergy to King Henry, in consequence, is well attested.

Henry's only ostensible purpose in summoning the Synod of Cashel was to make a pretense of carrying out the church reforms confided to him by the bulls, and his only real purpose was to secure, upon the strength of the bulls, the submission of as many of the political and religious leaders of the country as possible.

Strange indeed, if he failed to produce or mention documents from which he expected, and had good reason to expect, so much. He did produce them and the people were paralyzed by them. Just as the Roman populace was paralyzed with terror by the excommunication of the gallant Rienzi, who had led them in driving the plundering Orsini and Colonna families and their brigand followers from the Eternal City.

But the efforts of the Vatican in aid of King

Henry's conquest of Ireland did not end with the Synod of Cashel.

In the year 1177 a Synod was summoned in Dublin by, and was held under, Vivian, the Pope's Legate for Ireland.

"In this Synod," says Rev. P. J. Carew, Professor of Divinity in the Catholic College of Maynooth, Ireland (citing Dr. Lanigan's History), "the Legate set forth Henry's right to the sovereignty of Ireland, in virtue of the Pope's authority, and inculcated the necessity of obeying him *under pain of excommunication."**

Until that time the Catholic Churches were inviolable sanctuaries into which the hunted people might flee, and in which their lives were safe from murder and their property from spoliation. At this Synod of Dublin, the Pope through his Legate made Ireland an exception to this rule, and gave leave to the English soldiers to enter the churches and strip the people of the food brought there for safety.† Since these things were done by the Vicar of Christ, how terrible to contemplate what the Vicar of Hell would have done under similar circumstances.

---

* Carew's Ecclesiastical Hist. Ireland, p. 437 ; Walsh's Irish Hierarchy, p. 109; Dolby's Hist. Ireland, p. 31.
† Dolby's Hist., p. 31.

CHAPTER IV.
HUMILIATING THE IRISH PRIESTS AND PEOPLE.

In the year 1180 King Henry, "who persecuted the Holy Prelate, St. Lawrence, for his ardent attachment to the land of his birth, resolved that an office of so much importance (the Archbishopric of Dublin), should not be entrusted to an Irishman. * * Accordingly on the monarch's recommendation, his Chaplain, John Comyn, a native of England, was elected to the Archbishopric of Dublin, by some of the clergy who had assembled at Evesham for that purpose. *John was not then a priest*, but was in the following year ordained, and was consecrated by Pope Lucius III.," who, at the request of the King, released the new archbishop and his archdiocese from the control, and even from the visitations, of the Irish Primate of Ireland.*

From that time to the present—from Comyn to McCabe, at least—the British Government, as well since it became Protestant as while it was Catholic, has generally dictated, either directly or indirectly, the appointment of most of the Catholic archbishops and even bishops of Ireland. It became at one time a common saying that: "Ireland gets her rent receipts and archbishops from England."

---

* Walsh's Irish Hierarchy, p. 110; Dolby's Hist., p. 33;

Since the reformation, the government negotiations with the Vatican have been conducted by secret emissaries and are difficult of discovery, but occasionally an uncovered track is found which *discloses* something, and *indicates* a great deal more. For example, in a letter written by Lord Palmerston (then English secretary of foreign affairs) to his brother, May 12th, 1834, occurs the following : " I am sending off a messenger suddenly to Florence and to Rome to try to get the Pope not to appoint an agitating prelate Archbishop of Tuam, and I write a few lines by him to you, as he may as well go on to Naples from Rome while the Pope is pondering upon his answer."*

Greville's Memoirs shed further light on this subject. Speaking of Lord Melbourne (then Home Secretary under Grey's Administration) he says : " He told me that an application had been made to the Pope * * * * not to appoint McHale to the vacant Catholic bishopric. * * * * His Holiness said that he 'had remarked for a long time past that no piece of preferment of any value ever fell vacant in Ireland that he did not get an application from the British Government asking for the appointment.' Lord Melbourne, * * * * in reply to my question, admitted that *the Pope had generally conferred the*

---

* Evelyn Ashley's Life of Lord Palmerston; Chas. Gavan Duffy's Young Ireland, p. 211.

appointment according to the wishes of the Government." After commenting upon the "regular underhand intercourse" established between the Government and the Vatican and the constant solicitation of appointments from the Pope, he adds: *"the Pope,* who is the object of our orthodox abhorrence and dread, good-humoredly *complies with all, or nearly all, of their requests."**

On the 14th of September, 1808, the Catholic bishops of Ireland met in synod in Dublin and passed, among others, the following resolution: " That the Roman Catholic prelates pledge themselves to adhere to *the rules by which they have been hitherto uniformly guided*—namely, to *recommend* to his Holiness (for appointment as Irish Roman Catholic bishops) *only such persons as are of unimpeachable loyalty."†*

This accounts for the pro-English sentiments of so many Irish bishops, and accounts for the appointment of the Murrays, and Moriartys, and Cullens, and McCabes, and so on *ad nauseam, ad infinitum.*

But, enough; the story of the humiliation and degradation of Ireland's patriotic priests to the domination of Englishmen, Italians, Spaniards and

---

* Young Ireland, p. 211.
† Haverty's Hist., p. 746.

anti-Irish Irishmen is a long one, and interesting, but the studied attempt to degrade the Irish race, as such, is of more importance.

In the 13th and 14th centuries such race prejudices had arisen between the Irish and Anglo-Irish in Ireland that they each established rules, excluding the other from their canonries (religious colleges) and religious houses.

Complaint being made to Pope Innocent IV., he issued a bull requiring the Irish *to admit the English* and Anglo-Irish to their canonries.

Complaint being afterwards made by the Irish to Pope Leo X., he issued a bull confirming the right of the English *to exclude the Irish* from *their* canonries.*

Under this bull Irish ecclesiastics and students were excluded from institutions which had been founded and endowed by their own Irish ancestors.†

"Consistency, thou art a jewel," but, surely, Rome cannot be charged with inconsistency in dealing with the Irish. She has been consistently and constantly unjust and insulting to them.

She has found them confiding and obedient, while she has spurned and spat upon them, and

---

* Cambrensis Eversus, by Dr. Kelly, Vol. II., p. 543; Haverty's Hist., pp. 253-4, note.
† Haverty's Hist., p. 255.

she has spurned and spat upon them incessantly, apparently for no other reason than that she has found them *still* confiding and obedient, and that their humiliation pleased and conciliated a more independent power.

There is a general impression to the effect that the persecution of the Irish is due mainly to religious prejudice, but no man who has read deeply of Irish history can harbor such a delusion.

The English government and the Irish landlords (joint persecutors and plunderers of the race) care very little to what church an Irishman goes while living, or to what sphere his soul may be consigned after his death. The pretense to the contrary is a hollow sham, but it has a purpose. By dividing the people into hostile religious factions, and setting them to fight each other, the natural power of the Irish is greatly reduced, and the difficulty of perpetuating the enslavement of both factions is greatly lessened.

Besides, one of the factions would naturally ally itself to the Protestant Government of England, while the other would as naturally ally itself to the head of the Catholic Church. The Government and the Pope acting in concert through the "regular underhand intercourse" of which Greville speaks, and which Petre, Errington and Norfolk have so lately exemplified, the wisdom of the Government's promotion of religious feuds among the Irish people is apparent.

"It should not be forgotten that it has always been the policy of the English Government in Ireland to foment religious dissentions there as a powerful means of perpetuating its own dominion."*

That religious differences are not the cause of Irish persecution, is conclusively proved by the fact that the most cruel and barbarous persecution of the Irish people took place during and throughout the period of four hundred years before England became protestant; and while the Kings of England were the Pope's "beloved sons in Christ," as they were affectionately termed.

Speaking on this subject. Rev. R. A. Byrne, in a lecture on "The Free Schools of Ancient Ireland," pertinently said: "In 1380 it was enacted (at Downpatrick Abbey) that no mere Irishman should be allowed to make his profession in the Abbey.

This is but in keeping with the spirit of English *Catholic* domination in Ireland everywhere. This anti-Irish feeling is of no modern date, and by no means owes its origin to the introduction of Protestantism. Heny VIII. was a bad man . * *

---

* Ireland of To-day, by M. F. Sullivan, p. 369.

but *the deadly wounds that laid Erin low were struck by the assassin-hands of his Catholic forefathers."**

It was this same English Catholic spirit that animated that typical English priest, Monsignor Capel,† when he said at Metropolitan Hall, in this city, that, in his opinion, "the Irish famine of 1847-8 was a God's blessing."

Daniel O'Connell, in 1813, said "The English do not dislike us as Catholics; they simply hate us as Irish."‡

John Mitchell most happily and truly stated the situation when he said, that to England the material wealth of the Irish was "far more valuable than their souls."

But the English Protestant people, as a people, where they are even partially free from the influence of caste, which affects both Protestants and Catholics alike, and from that hydra-headed monster of bigotry, which in both countries is miscalled religion, have no such prejudice against the Irish race. This was well proved during the years of famine, when "the good will of the English people" was shown by their subscription of more than two million dollars, to relieve the distress of

---
* Ireland as She Is, by J. J. Clancy, p. 82.
† "Domestic Prelate to His Holiness Pope Leo XIII." THE POPE, p. 1.
‡ Ireland as She Is, p. 80.

the Irish; some, at least, of the English people, going even without butter on their bread, "in order that some money might be saved for the starving poor of Ireland."*

It is therefore not to English *Catholics* nor to Italian *Catholics* that Ireland must look for sympathy and succor in her struggle for political liberty and civil justice, but to the lovers of Liberty and Justice, of all shades of religious belief, throughout the world.

She has been sadly handicapped in her struggle, by her dependence on the broken reed of Roman honor.

I must close this prolific branch of my subject with one more general statement and a couple of historical examples.

Under all "their Catholic Majesties," from Henry II. to Henry VIII. (nearly 400 years), the Irish people, with the exception of five families, were outlaws. They were murdered at will, like dogs, by their English Catholic neighbors in Ireland, and there was no law to punish the murderers.†

Yet, during all of this unparalleled reign of terror, history fails to show a single instance in which

---

* The Parnell Movement, by T. P. O'Connor, p. 117.
† Ireland as She Is, pp. 18 to 27 and citations.

the power of the Catholic Church was ever exerted or suggested, by any pope, for the protection of her faithful Irish children.

In the year 1311, for example, and as a mere illustration of the esteem in which Irish lives were held by these Catholic princes: "Wm. Fritz Roger, being arraigned for the felonious slaying of Roger de Cantelon, comes and says, he could not commit felony by means of such killing, because the aforesaid Roger (de Cantelon) was an Irishman and not of free blood. And the jury upon their oath say that the aforesaid Roger *was* an Irishman, and *therefore* the said William as far as regards the said felony is acquitted." *

But as the aforesaid Roger was found to be *an Irishman belonging to the King*, the unlucky murderer was "recommitted to jail, until he shall find pledges to pay five marks† to our Lord the King, *for the value of the aforesaid Irishman.*"‡

I suppose this penalty was imposed under some of the English laws against poaching, but as to that, I am not prepared to make a positive statement, and do not deem the subject of sufficient importance for investigation, since the fine was

---

* Davies' Hist. Tracts, p. 78, et. seq.; Ireland as She Is, p. 20; Dolby's Hist., p. 58.
† About $16.50.
‡ Dolby's Hist., p. 58.

manifestly not imposed for the protection of the lives of Irishmen, but merely to preserve them as chattels of the King.

In 1465 an act was passed (indirectly but effectually) giving rewards for the killing of Irishmen, just as with us rewards are given for the killing of coyotes;* and the marriage, fostering, gossip and trade of English Catholics with Irish Catholics, were made penal offenses by Catholic parliaments and Catholic kings.* Under these laws, murders innumerable—causeless, cruel, sportive murders—were committed with impunity. Through their bishops, archbishops, primates and legates the popes must have been fully advised concerning these atrocities; the English rulers and people were Catholics, and as much subject to the popes as the Irish now are; yet there was no excommunication and no threat of excommunication, by any of the popes, against the English for their hellish practices. But assuming that all of the pope's legitimate advisers in Ireland were such scoundrels and conspirators with the kings, upon whose favor their offices depended, yet the plea of ignorance could not be made for the popes.

O'Neill, King of Ulster, and other Irish princes,

---
* Ireland as She Is, p. 21.
† Ireland as She Is, p. 20.

fully represented those grievances to Pope John XXII., who paid no attention to them for more than twelve years, when, at last, he sent a letter to King Edward III., mildly advising that monarch to adopt a different policy and to reform the evils as speedily as possible. On what ground? Solely on the ground of expediency; namely: "lest it might be too late hereafter to apply a remedy when the spirit of revolt has grown stronger."*

If he had been dealing with the Irish he would have sent a bull commanding them to desist within a fixed time on pain of excommunication, but the English, although Catholics, were not so much afraid of bulls as were the Irish. Hence their milder treatment.

Hence the Vatican, now so anxious to shield the enemies and plunderers of the Irish people from peaceful ostracism (boycotting), never lifted the scepter of Church authority to shield the Irish from wanton murder, outrage and robbery, when those crimes, through centuries, were being perpetrated by the English Catholic children of the Church.†

---

* Haverty's Hist., pp. 255–6.

† King John of England was excommunicated by Pope Innocent III., in the year 1208, while the former was engaged in murdering the Irish and devastating parts of their country; but the excommunication had nothing to do with his persecution of the Irish. It grew out of the Pope's refusal to

The whole history of the Vatican shows that ever since it assumed to be the political as well as the religious head of the world (about the year 860),* its universal policy has been to crush the weak; to frighten the timid and to conciliate the strong and defiant.

Acting on this policy, and finding the Irish people afraid of papal wrath, each succeeding pope has traded for political and other advantages with England on the strength of his power to coerce and subdue the Irish people.

---

appoint the King's nominee as Archbishop of Canterbury, and the King's refusal to allow Stephen Langdon, whom the Pope appointed, to act in that capacity. The Pope having frightened the King by inviting the Catholic powers of Europe to invade England, this trouble was compromised. The King agreeing to accept Langdon as Archbishop and to lay his crown at the feet of Cardinal Pandulf, the Pope's Legate, who, after kicking it contemptuously, replaced it on the King's head. Henry VIII. and Queen Elizabeth, both cruel enemies of Ireland, were also excommunicated: the first by Pope Paul III., in 1535, and the latter by Pope Pius V., in 1570; but it is needless to say that these excommunications grew out of troubles connected with the Protestant Reformation, and had nothing to do with the persecution of Ireland.—J. G. M.

* Catholic Dictionary, Addis and Arnold, Tit. "Tiara."

CHAPTER V.

PAPAL INTERFERENCE WITH IRISH STRUGGLES FOR LIBERTY AFTER THE CONQUEST.

Many Irish historians are specially severe in their strictures on Adrian IV., "the only Englishman who ever occupied the Papal throne," as if he were the only pope who had ever interfered with the political liberties of the Irish people, but the acts of his successors are not a whit less iniquitous.

I have already mentioned the bull of Pope Alexander III., confirming the grant of Adrian, and the action of his Legate at the Synod of Dublin in 1177, wherein he threatened the excommunication of such of the Irish people as refused to recognize the right of King Henry to the sovereignty of Ireland.

I have also referred to the appointment, by the popes, of English and pro-English bishops, archbishops, primates and legates to rule over the church in Ireland.

These prelates deemed it a part of their duty, no doubt a pleasant part, to bless the loyal English and to curse the rebellious Irish, in the name of the Catholic Church, in all controversies between the races.

But, so strong was the love of liberty among the Irish people (said to have been the growth of thirty centuries),* that the ban of the local church dignitaries was not sufficient to restrain it; and, even in the 14th century, England was obliged to call for special interference from the Vatican.

In the year 1315, after the memorable Scottish victory on the field of Bannockburn, the princes and popular leaders of the Irish people invited Edward Bruce (brother of Robert Bruce) to enter Ireland and make common cause with them in their struggle for liberty. Accordingly, on May 25th of that year, Bruce landed in Ireland with six thousand veterans. These were at once joined by the Irish armies of Ulster. Castles were stormed, cities were burned, "and," says the historian, "in a very short space of time, no trace of the English remained in Ulster but the desolation of their former dwellings."†

Felim O'Connor, King of Connaught (whose "dignity and possessions had been restored to him by the English"), deserted the English and cast his fortunes with the advancing armies of

---

* O'Halloran's Hist., p. 19.
† Dolby's Hist., p. 58.

O'Neill and Bruce. "The O'Briens of Thomond, and a great proportion of the toparchs of Munster and Meath (then a province), followed his example." Their victorious armies swept over Ossory and entered Munster. Here they met with some reverses. English supremacy in Ireland had reached a crisis, and, in the supreme moment, England turned to Pope John XXII. "The English interest soon began to revive, and the Pope lent his powerful assistance to restore its ascendancy. Sentence of excommunication was solemnly pronounced against Bruce and all his adherents."*

Then followed the famous battle of Dundalk, which sealed the fate of Ireland for all the succeeding centuries. The Pope's decree presided as a grim spectre over the battle. "*The Irish felt that they fought under the curse of the church;* while the English were roused by the belief that Heaven was on their side, and that the *blessing pronounced on their arms by the Primate*, that very morning, rendered them invincible."†

"Under the curse of the church!" Yes, every battle for Ireland's liberty and for natural justice to her plundered people, has been fought under

---
* Dolby's Hist., p. 59.
† Dolby's Hist., p. 60.

the curse of the church. The gallant Irish, who never shrank from the whistling bullets or the cold steel of their armed foes, have always withered and failed under the blighting breath of Roman curses.

"How long, O Lord! how long",will the Irish people stand divided between two opinions concerning the Pope's authority to keep them in political thraldom?

So complete and demoralizing was the English victory at Dundalk, and so crushing was the vengence dealt out to the surviving leaders and helpless people, that the Pope's personal services were not again required by England in maintaining the subjection of Ireland prior to the reformation (1534).

CHAPTER VI.

THE RELIGIOUS WARS.

The religious rupture between England and the Vatican, following the abolition of Papal authority in English territory, led Pope Clement VIII. to foster the Irish rebellion of 1598—not for the purpose of freeing Ireland, but for the purpose of securing from England better terms for the church—and accordingly in the year following, he sent with Oviedo, a Spaniard whom he had appointed Archbishop of Dublin, a number of indulgences, with power to grant other indulgences, "*to those of the Irish who fought against the English in defense of the ancient religion.*"*

In the year 1643 Father Scarampi came to Ireland as the Legate of Pope Urban VIII., bearing "a bull of indulgences to the Irish Catholics; and he also brought with him from Father Wadding (representative of the Catholic Confederates of Ireland, at the Vatican) a sum of $30,000, with a quantity of arms and ammunition."†

The insurrection of 1641 was then in progress, but this uprising was not a struggle for Irish nationality nor for the political emancipation of the Irish people. Its purpose was to secure "a partial transfer of property, and certain stipulations in favor of the Church of Rome,"‡ the most radical demand by the insurgents being "perfect *religious* liberty."‖

It was directed and governed by "The Supreme Council of the Confederate Catholics of Ireland,"§

---

* Dolby's Hist., p. 238; Haverty's Hist., p. 437.
† Haverty's Hist., p. 502.
‡ Haverty's Hist., pp. 480, 508, 517-18.
‖ Haverty's Hist., p. 501.
§ Haverty's Hist., p. 491.

and was encouraged not only by the Pope but also by the Catholic nations of Europe, especially France and Spain.*

I dwell upon these details not for the purpose of belittling the movement, nor to discredit the Pope's services, but to show that in its true character it was a religious war between Catholic Europe and Protestant England, of which Ireland was the battle ground, in which the Pope was equally interested with the Irish people, and that, as in the struggle of 1598, the Irish armies, while fighting for the grand and just and holy principle of religious liberty at home, were really helping the Pope far more than they were being helped by him. It may be justly said to have been essentially his war, since, by abandoning him, all the immunities claimed by the Irish would have been promptly secured to them.

In 1645 Pope Innocent X., continuing the policy of his predecessor, sent a nuncio to the Council of the Confederate Catholics, and also sent a few men, a little money, some munitions and implements of war, and one ship, to aid them in the struggle against religious persecution and anti-Catholic penal laws.†

---

* Haverty's Hist., p. 502-7.
† Haverty's Hist., p. 507.

These religious feuds necessarily estranged the English Government from the Vatican for at least two centuries, and apparently for a much longer period. But none may know when or how the subsequently discovered "regular underhand intercourse"* was established, for it appears that, even in the midst of this war, King Charles I. had an emissary (Lord Herbert) in secret conference with the papal nuncio (Father Rinuccini) with the knowledge, however, of the Catholic Council, but unknown to the regular representatives of his own government. So that when an attempt was made to negotiate a peace, the Catholic clergy were "secretly acquainted with the intention of the King to grant much more than Ormond (Lord Lieutenant) stipulated for."† It would seem that very little affecting Ireland for good or evil was done by the Vatican from the close of this war until the beginning of the present century.

---

* See p. 28.
† Haverty's Hist., pp. 505–6.

CHAPTER VII.

A SOP TO CERBERUS.

In the year 1795 a most extraordinary, but keen, far-sighted and statesmanlike change was made by the English Government in the matter of governing the restless, liberty-craving Irish.

The preceding generations of religious persecution had blended in the minds of the Irish people the trials of the Catholic church and its priesthood with the wrongs of their race.* The priests (a brave, noble and patriotic body of teachers and comforters), had become their traditional advisers in politics as well as in religious matters. No priesthood in the world was ever nearer to the hearts of its people, and none was ever more deservedly beloved. Though severe in discipline, they were kind, generous and attentive and in full sympathy with the national aspirations of the people. Edmund Burke, Wm. Pitt, Lord Granville, Chas. J. Fox and other English statesmen resolved upon a plan, acceptable to the Vatican, and also to the Irish bishops and representatives, by which the great influence of the Irish priesthood might

---

* Mc'Carthy's Hist. of Our Own Times, Vol. IV, pp. 190 to 196.

be made, at least negatively, to serve the purposes of the English Government.

This plan was no less than the establishment of a royal college for the education of Irish Catholic priests at the expense of the English Protestant Government.

Accordingly, in that year the Pitt ministry "recommended the Irish Parliament to appropriate a grant of eight thousand pounds ($40,000) per annum, to support a college for the education of the Irish priesthood,"* and that sum was thereupon appropriated for the maintenance of the Catholic Theological College of Maynooth.

In the year 1807 (after the Union) this grant was increased by the British Parliament to £13,000 ($65,000) per annum.

The purpose was to educate for the priesthood, in this college, the sons of the common people of all parts of Ireland; to educate them out of "the Irish idea" into a sort of patriotic conservatism. The idea was not to make them pro-English, nor even unpatriotic, for that would destroy their very valuable influence with the people, but it was to make them more Catholic than Irish, eager to struggle for Ireland when unrestrained, but ready to sacrifice the cause of Ireland to the cause of the

---

* Mooney's Hist., p. 1535.

church, or to church discipline, at any moment, upon the call of their religious superiors.

The priests so selected and educated were to be distributed through all the 2,500 parishes of Ireland, at least one being assigned to each parish.

The strength and elasticity of this new scheme of religio-political government must be at once apparent. This great body of pro-Irish priests, moving and sympathizing with the people, yet bound to an absolute obedience, to a small body of pro-English bishops, selected for their "unimpeachable loyalty"* to the English Government and all controlled as absolutely as if they were automatons by an Italian pontiff,† the latter (generally a member of the Italian nobility, or *noblesse* —a most important fact—as I will presently show), being in league with the British Government through unofficial, but all powerful, secret ambassadors.

This was the scheme,‡ and from all that we can glean from the pages of Irish history, the Vatican and the government seem to have been in full accord concerning it.

Its immediate success was greatly hindered by

---

* See p. 28.

† "In his subjects the Holy Father has inculcated the union of all hearts in the cause of Holy Church; * * * a loyal obedience of people to pastors, and of people and pastors to the Holy See." (The Pope, by Monsignor Capel, Domestic Prelate of his Holiness Pope Leo XIII., p. 38.

‡ See pp. 53-5.

the hostility or indifference of those who succeeded to the control of public affairs after the increased grant of 1807, but the college endowment did not cease to form a strong bond of union between the government and the Vatican.

The strength of this bond may be surmised from the fact that the Vatican favored a public statute, giving the English Protestant government a voice in the selection of Irish Catholic bishops. My authority for this statement is that in 1810 the English Catholics charged the Irish with "wavering in their allegiance to the pope" because they opposed the measure,* and in 1814 published a rescript from Pope Pius VII., expressly recommending that concession. Daniel O'Connell, subsequently (in 1832), speaking of this period said: "the Catholic laity were totally repugnant to *allow the crown any power to nominate the Catholic bishops of Ireland.*

We steadily opposed the Court of Rome, as well as the inclination shown by our own prelates; we resolutely resisted the wishes of our nobility, and of so many of our merchants, backed as they were by the almost universal voice of the Catholics of England."†

In view of the secret relations of the govern-

---
* Haverty's Hist., p. 748.
† Haverty's Hist., p. 761.

ment and the Vatican, as subsequently discovered, this measure seems to have been unimportant, since the government already enjoyed the secret privilege of doing all that the act contemplated.

CHAPTER VIII.

THE REPEAL MOVEMENT KILLED BY A RESCRIPT.

In the year 1829, O'Connell organized the great Repeal movement, which has immortalized his name, and which gave such bright promise of fulfilling the last prayer of the illustrious Emmet. It grew with amazing rapidity. Around the leader gathered a grand galaxy of statesmen, poets, and orators, whose words and works cast an imperishable luster over Erin's race, and lent a new dignity to the character of man. The people of Ireland believed in them and flocked, not in thousands, nor in tens of thousands merely, but in hundreds of thousands, to their meetings, eager to learn the gospel of political deliverance from their lips. The tide of this political movement rose and rolled with majestic power. Reform after reform was accomplished. Proposition after proposition was made by the English Government. Anything short of a total repeal of the Union could be had by the Irish for the asking; and even repeal, with broader, better, happier conditions than those that had been lost by the Union, seemed almost within reach. O'er the long-watched horizon of hope deferred, the sunburst of freedom was breaking. But lo! the Goddess of Irish Liberty, lately so joyful, is weeping. She faints, she reels! What evil fortune has befallen her? Alas! the fangs of the Vatican serpent have been driven again to her heart. The learned and patriotic priesthood of Ireland had become the teachers and leaders of the people of this movement, in every parish. Pope Gregory XVI., in the year 1843, "at the urgent instigation of the British Ministry, through the Austrian Ambassador at Rome, and through the more direct agency of a Mr. Petre, who, it appears, had acted on behalf of England at the Court of the Holy See " * issued a *rescript* commanding the priests of Ireland to refrain from attending the repeal meetings. This treacherous and unexpected blow had a stunning effect upon the movement. It silenced at once thousands of its active and trusted leaders.

It was as if all the commissioned officers of their mighty army had been captured at once by the enemy.

O'Connell saw in this *rescript* the doom of his

---

* Mooney's Hist., Vol. II., p. 1530.

KILLED BY A RESCRIPT.   51

race and country; the blasting of all his cherished hopes.

He rose in the grandeur of his almost superhuman power to meet and turn the blow of the Holy See. He published a letter to prove that the rescript was an illegal interference with the civil liberties of the clergy.* In the agony of his soul be uttered his famous cry: *"As much religion as you please from Rome, but no politics."*

He called upon the clergy to stand by the movement and they did, at least mechanically, respond. Mooney thereupon says: "The clergy are as much repealers as they ever were, and the current of agitation goes on quite as steadily and powerfully as before the document was issued."†

Alas! the events prove the contrary. During the paralysis, which resulted from the blow, the fatal decay of disentegration had set in.

The priests came forward as before, but not with the firm step and earnest purpose of their former enthusiasm. They wavered between love of country and vows of obedience. The mighty movement, then in its prime,‡ which had grown and flourished and triumphed for fifteen years, withered and died. Within three years from the

---
* Mooney's Hist., pp. 1530–1.
† Mooney's Hist., p. 1531,
‡ Haverty's Hist., 786–7.

date of the rescript it had joined the empire of the eternal past.

Poor O'Connell, most faithful son of the Church, truest friend of the Vatican, he must have felt most keenly:

> "How colder than the wind that freezes,
> Founts that but now in sunshine played,
> Is the congealing pang which seizes
> The trusting bosom when betrayed."

He died at Genoa of a broken heart on May 15th, 1847, and strangely willed his heart* to the destroyers of his life and his country.†

THE PRICE OF THE RESCRIPT.

What was the consideration which moved the Vatican to issue the rescript?

As it was the result of secret negotiations, the details of which have never been directly published or made known, it is impossible to say, authoritatively, what was its price; but certain it is that shortly before and shortly after its issuance the British Government made legislative concessions to the Church which were most pleasing to the Vatican.

The first was the repeal of the obnoxious stat-

---

* The Parnell Movement, p. 69.

† It is but just to his memory to state that he was then suffering from softening of the brain, superinduced by the mental agony involved in witnessing the dying struggles of his cherished movement. Young Ireland, p. 531; the Parnell Movement, p. 13.

ute of Mortmain, in 1842. The repeal of this law was a just and proper measure, and was generally supposed to have been forced from the government by the Repeal Association, but, in the light of events following so closely after it, there may be some force in the suggestion that it was in part the *result* of the repeal agitation and in part the price of its destruction.

The other concession was an act of Parliament passed in 1845, increasing the grant to Maynooth College from £13,000 to £26,000 ($130,000) per annum, and making an additional appropriation of £30,000 ($150,000) for the enlargement of its buildings.

Speaking of this grant, Mr. Thomas Power O'Connor says: " Sir Robert Peel, by the concession of a larger grant to Maynooth, still further disintegrated the forces of O'Connell by bringing pressure on the Vatican, and, through the Vatican, on some of the bishops; and so O'Connell's power began gradually to melt away." *

On the passage of this act, Richard Lalor Shiel, Catholic member of Parliament for Dungarvan, who had discredited his patriotism by accepting an appointment to office under the

---

* Parnell Movement, p. 15.

English Government,* made a most remarkable speech, openly avowing, reviewing, and enforcing the purposes of the original College grant, of which it may not be uninteresting to quote a few passages here: "You are taking a step in the right direction," he said. "You are advancing in a career of which you have left the starting post far behind, and of which the goal perhaps is not far distant. You must not take the Catholic clergy into your pay, *but you can take the Catholic Church under your care.* * * * Maynooth was founded in a great measure at the suggestion of the apostle of order, the great Edmund Burke. Let him be assured that he has made great progress in *the art of governing Ireland,* by whom the works of Edmund Burke are perused with admiration. That sagacious man saw that it was not to the interest of Protestant England that the priesthood of Catholic Ireland should be educated in France; he thought that evils could arise from a French and Irish ecclesiastical fraternization; he did not wish that French principles should be imported into every Irish parish, and he denounced the introduction of a Gallo-Hibernian establishment into Ireland. Edmund Burke was of opinion that *the Irish Catholic priesthood should be educated by the state and for the state.*

---

* Parnell Movement, p. 76.

Give the Catholic priest and the Irish Protestant proprietor a common interest in maintaining the institutions of their country and their reconciliation will be immediate and complete. Indeed the only danger to be apprehended is, that their alliance may become too unqualified and too compact. * * * * Great ability will be allured into Maynooth—gold for genius has a magnetic power. * * * Locate in every parish an educated Catholic priest, whose mind has undergone the process of literary refinement, and you will accomplish much in the way of national amelioration. * * * Even if the sum to be granted were five times what the minister recommends you to concede, there is so much true economy in the results of wise legislation that your very love of saving should induce you to act with liberality to Ireland. *Are not lectures at Maynooth cheaper than State prosecutions? Are not professors less costly than crown solicitors? Is not a large standing army, and a great constabulary force, more expensive than the moral police with which, by the priesthood of Ireland, you can be thriftily and efficaciously supplied?*"*

Why did Shiel suppose that the priests educated at Maynooth would render the same service for

---

* Shiel's Speeches, by MacNevin, p. 338, et seq.

England that had previously been rendered by state prosecutors, crown solicitors, the standing army, and the constabulary force?

Why did the English Government believe the promise and make the grant?

There can be but one answer. The English Government, then in secret diplomatic correspondence with the Vatican,* had satisfactory assurances that none but pro-English bishops and archbishops would be appointed for Ireland, and that, by educating her priesthood into a sufficiently rigid political subserviency to their religious superiors, they might readily be made the unconscious instruments of English tyranny, and might ultimately aid in eliminating the spirit of nationality from the Irish character.

These, at least, were the hopes and expectations of the English Government, and, if they have in anything failed, the failure has certainly not been the fault of the Vatican or its Anglo-Irish bishops, as we shall see.

---

* See p. 28.

CHAPTER IX.

YOUNG IRELAND MOVEMENT KILLED BY BISHOPS AND PRIESTS.

When the repeal movement passed away, the spirit of Irish nationality was represented by the Young Ireland Party—"the men of '48."

Of this party the illustrious Alexander M. Sullivan says: "They were pre-eminently the party of religious tolerance. The leading idea, in what may be called their home policy, was to break down the antagonism between Catholics and Protestants in Ireland."*

The following lines, from the pen of the immortal Thomas Davis, well illustrates the noble and truly fraternal spirit of the movement:

> "What matter that at different shrines
> We pray unto one God?
> What matter that at different times
> Our fathers won this sod?
> In fortune and in name were bound
> By stronger links than steel;
> And neither can be safe or sound
> But in the other's weal.
> * * * * *
> And oh, it were a gallant deed
> To show, before mankind,
> How every race and every creed
> Might be by love combined—
> Might be combined, yet not forget
> The fountains whence they rose,
> As filled by many a rivulet
> The stately Shannon flows."

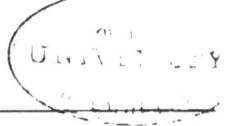

---

* New Ireland, p. 98.

Equally grand, liberal and inspiring was his famous "Orange and Green," addressed to his fellow Protestants of Ulster, in which these lines occur:

> "Freedom fled us;
> Knaves misled us;
> Under the feet of the foeman we lay;
> But in their spite
> The Irish unite
> For Orange and Green will carry the day."

In like strain wrote also those glorious daughters of Erin: "Eva,"* "Mary,"† and "Speranza."‡ In one of the last poems of "Speranza," published in the *Nation*, occurs the following:

> "We are blind, not discerning the promise,
> 'Tis the sword of the spirit that kills;
> Give us light and the fetters fall from us,
> For the strong soul is free when it wills."

Did these lines have reference to the subject which I am now discussing?

In vain, in vain! all, all in vain! Again, as at Dundalk, the champions of Irish liberty "fought under the curse of the Church."

The Catholic clergy set themselves invincbily against the movement.

Quoting again from Sullivan, who was an

---

* Eva Mary Kelly, afterwards Mrs. Kevin O'Dougherty.

† Ellen Downing. She died of grief, on being discarded by Joe Brennan, her patriot lover.

‡ Jane Frances Eglee, daughter of a Protestant minister; now Lady Wilde and mother of Oscar Wilde.

active participant, and, at the same time, an earnest Catholic, and even an extreme Ultramontane (being one of the chief organizers of the "Irish Brigade" for the Pope's army in 1860),* we find : "At this time, in 1848, the power of the Catholic priests was unbroken—was stronger than ever. The famine scenes, in which their love for the people was attested by heroism and self sacrifice such as the world had never seen surpassed, had given them an influence which none could question or withstand. Their antagonism was fatal to the movement—more surely and infallibly fatal to it than all the power of the British Crown."†

The famine-years undoubtedly called forth the noblest traits of all true characters. All honor to the Catholic priests for having done their priestly duty so nobly in that awful period, but it should be remembered that many of their Protestant brethren of the cloth were also self-sacrificing. Of this the following instance, given by Mr. Sullivan, is a striking example:

"The Protestant curate of my native parish, in 1847, was the Rev. Alexander Ben Hallowell,

---
* New Ireland, pp. 277 to 286.

† New Ireland, p. 119; John Mitchell says: "About the year 1850 Ireland became thoroughly subjugated, without almost a hope of escape. Everything was fitted to the hand of her enemy, and that enemy made most unrelenting use of the advantage. The Catholic bishops counselled obedience and submission." Hist. Ireland, Vol. II, p. 252.

subsequently rector of Clonakilty, and now I believe residing somewhere in Lancashire. There were comparatively few of his own flock in a way to suffer from the famine, but he dared death daily in his efforts to save the perishing creatures around him. A poor hunchback, named Richard O'Brien, lay dying of the plague in a deserted hovel at a place called 'The Custom Gap.' Mr. Hallowell passing by heard the moans and went in. A shocking sight met his view. On some rotten straw, in a dark corner, lay poor 'Dick' naked, except a few rags across his body. Mr. Hallowell rushed to the door and saw a young friend on the road. ' Run, run with this shilling and buy me some wine,' he cried. Then he re-entered the hovel, stripped off his own clothes, and with his own hands put upon the plague-stricken hunchback the flannel vest and drawers and shirt of which he had just divested himself. *I know this to be true. I was the 'young friend' who went for and brought the wine."**

Noble priests! noble ministers! Surely none of such men will be cast out of Heaven for making a mistake in the selection of his creed!

But why did this devoted Irish Catholic priesthood destroy the "Young Ireland" movement?

---

* New Ireland, p. 91.

It is said in their defense that "they regarded the Young Irelanders with suspicion." That: "They fancied they saw in this movement too much that was akin to the work of the continental revolutionists, and, greatly as they disliked the domination of England, they would prefer it a thousand times to such 'liberty' as the carbonari would proclaim."*

If I could believe that the Irish Catholic clergy acted in good faith on their own judgment, even on this ridiculously mistaken opinion of the "Young Irelanders," I would not feel privileged to say one word in denunciation of their conduct; for, as Irishmen, each had an unquestionable right, according to his honest judgment, to favor or oppose any movement affecting the political liberty of his country.

But I cannot believe that they opposed the movement for any such reason nor upon their independent judgment.

They knew that the movement was led by great and gifted statesmen, who fully realized their responsibility, and who, in public and in private,† opposed the methods of the carbonari and of the continental revolutionists. They knew also that

---
* New Ireland, p. 119.
† See letter of Gavan Duffy to Wm. Smith O'Brien, from Newgate Prison. New Ireland, p. 117.

neither the French Revolution then in progress, nor even the "carnival of fire and blood" which reigned in France at the close of the last century, could add one terror to the sufferings which the Irish people had endured and were enduring.

The artificial famine produced by English misgovernment and landlord avarice was still upon them, and held them in its torturing grasp.

On the combination rack of landlord-bred famine and famine-bred fever, the Irish people, in tens of thousands, were dying in agony, homeless and shelterless, in sight of the cabins which their own hands or the hands of their ancestors had built, but from which inhuman landlordism had evicted them, in their hour of direst affliction. They were hungering to death in sight of granaries filled with fruits which the God-given soil of Ireland had yielded to the inspiration of their own toil, but which, under the malign power of English laws, they had been compelled to surrender to idle landlords.

These landlords had, and have, no purpose in living, save that of collecting toll from their industrious fellow-men; giving absolutely nothing in return except a superfluous assent to their victims' God-given privilege of using the natural resources of their native land.

Justin McCarthy, an eye witness, speaking of this period (1847 to 1857), says: "Evictions took place by the hundred, by the thousand, by the ten thousand—evictions as much for grazier's purposes as for non-payment of rent, which in those evil days of famine and failure they could not pay. Winter or summer, day or night, fair or foul weather, the tenants were ejected. Sick or well, bed-ridden or dying, the tenants—men, women or children—were turned out. They might go to America if they could; they might die on the roadside, if so it pleased them. They were out of the hut, and the hut was unroofed that they might not seek its shelter again, and that was all the landlord cared about."*

These evictors and their allies, bear in mind, are the hell-hounds whom the Holy Father (?) is now so eager to shield from peaceful ostracism and legal embarrassments at the hands of their victims.

There was not even a scarcity of food in Ireland during the years of famine, but only a failure of the immediate crops on which the plundered *tenantry* depended.†

---

* Ireland since the Union, p. 141.

† "The harvest of 1847 was also very abundant in Ireland, and it was one of the deadliest years of famine. The English offered thanksgivings to God for the Irish harvests, and then devoured them," Mitchell's Hist., Vol. II, p. 252.

Mrs. Nicholson, another eye witness, in her soul-harrowing work, "Lights and Shades of Ireland," says: "What shall be said of the pitiful landlords, who were still drinking their wine, while pouring their doleful complaints into government's ears, that no rents were paid. * * * * But these afflicted landlords were exporting to the continent vast quantities of grain, which their poor starving tenants had labored to produce. They were not allowed to eat a morsel of their food, but must buy it from others or starve."*

And again. "Next to the absurdity of Cork and Limerick exporting cargoes of Irish grain for sale, and at the same time receiving cargoes of American grain to be given away at the cost of the English people, may be ranked the folly, if it may not properly be called by some worse name, of seeing hundreds dying for want of food, at the same time permitting the conversion of *as much grain as would feed the whole of those dying of starvation, and many more*, into a fiery liquid which * * * * never saved a single life or improved a single character."†

Was this abject poverty of the Irish tenantry due to idleness or improvidence? No. In years

---
* pp. 30–1.
† Lights and Shades, p. 130.

of plenty as well as in years of scarcity the tenant is robbed of all the fruits of his labor, except that in good years he is left a slave's portion, enough to keep body and soul together.

Industry, providence and self-sacrifice are and were the general characteristics of the Irish peasantry. One illustration, among thousands that I might cite, must here suffice. It is also from the pen of Mrs. Nicholson. She had been riding on a car on which a tattered and repulsive looking man was also seated. On alighting from the car this man fell prostrate in the passage. She found that his weakness "was exhaustion, occasioned by hunger," and thus proceeds: "When he could speak in a whisper, he begged Mrs. Arthur to take a few sovereigns which he had sewed in his ragged coat, and send them to his wife and children, who were suffering for food. He had been at work in England, and, knowing the dreadful state his family were in at home, had saved a few sovereigns, not willing to break one, and endeavored to reach home on a few shillings he had, and being so weak for want of food he occasionally rode a few miles when it rained and had not eaten once in two days."*

It is to be hoped that the poor wife and children

---

* Lights and Shades, p. 119.

obtained the money without the knowledge of the landlord's factor, as, otherwise, it must surely have gone to buy wine for the landlord instead of food for them.

This spirit of self-sacrifice was not confined to mothers and fathers : " It is *expected* that mothers will suffer and even die for their famishing little ones, if needful ; but to see children suffer for one another, was magnanimity above all. Two houseless, starving little orphan boys," says Mrs. Nicholson, "one about nine and the other five, called at the door of a rich widow of my acquaintance and asked for food. The woman had consumed all her bread at breakfast but a small piece, and giving this to the eldest she said : You must divide this with your little brother: I have no more." She then tells us that the lady "looked after them unperceived" and saw the elder boy give the whole piece to the other, and turn away to stifle the pangs of his own hunger while his weaker companion devoured it.*

And these, bear in mind incidentally, are the people from whom the present Pope, by the spiritual terror and coercion of his rescript, seeks to take away the only effective peaceful weapons of self-defense that they have ever had against the

---
* Lights and Shades, p. 120.

murderous and thrice damnable institution of landlordism.

Everywhere throughout the Island these scenes appeared, shocking the sight, freezing the souls and haunting the memories of beholders, and all produced directly by the two institutions against which the gallant Young Irelanders were contending.

With the white lips, the glassy eyes and the bony fingers of gaunt visaged famine thus everywhere pleading for succor or death, what had Ireland to fear from "the methods of the continental revolutionists?" Absolutely nothing.

Why then did the priesthood oppose the only movement that had for its object the removal of the causes, or any of the causes, of this artificial famine and this systematic plunder of the industrious by the idle?

My answer is, that they must have been acting under orders from the Pope and the bishops.

John Mitchell says: "The Catholic bishops counseled obedience and submission" to the English Government,* and we know that the bishops, besides being appointed for their "unimpeachable loyalty," are directed largely by secret orders from the Vatican, which they are sworn to keep secret even

---

* Mitchell's Hist., Vol. II, p. 252.

from the priests of their jurisdictions. In such cases the orders of the Pope are issued to the priests and people as if they originated with the bishops.

Assuming that, if the Pope did directly bring his authority to bear on the Irish bishops,* and through them on the priests and people to destroy the Young Ireland movement, his action must have been induced by some consideration moving from the English Government, I immediately looked for acts of Parliament relating to the church and the Vatican.

Strangely enough, I find that in the year 1848 —the pivotal year of the Young Ireland struggle —a political privilege which had previously been denied for over three hundred years, was accorded to the Pope by an act of Parliament.†

By this act the Government was authorized to re-open diplomatic relations with the Pope and to receive, in regal state, a papal ambassador at the Court of St. James.

To those not familiar with the history of the Vatican, since it has fallen under the absolute dominion of what has been most aptly called "the Italian Ring," this may seem a small price to en-

---
* Parnell's Movement, p. 15.
† Stats. 11 and 12, Vict. (1848), Chap. 108, p. 686.

gage the head of the Catholic Church in assisting to perpetuate the bondage of six millions of faithful Catholics,* but to those who have read and watched the political history and movements of that ring, the sufficiency of the consideration will be quite apparent.

Those who have observed the painful eagerness with which the cardinals and popes—" the princes"† and "supreme rulers of the world" ‡— have bent "the pregnant hinges of their knees," and extended their hands, for small political favors, from the temporal rulers of European nations, will realize the tremendous importance attached by the Vatican to this recognition at the English Court.‖

This act constitutes the missing link and completes the chain of causation. It makes plain the fact, and the reason, that the Vatican required the Irish priesthood to oppose the Young Ireland movement. The English Government had purchased its support and the *quid pro quo* must be given.

---
* The sad remnant of the eight millions of two years before; Hist. of Our Own Times, Vol. I, p. 324.

† "The rank of Cardinal, in its temporal aspect, is equivalent to that of a reigning prince. On their seals they have their own arms, with the red hat as crest." Catholic Dictionary, Tit. "Cardinal," p. 120.

‡ Catholic Dictionary, Tit. "Tiara," p. 796.

‖ For the enlightenment of those to whom this knowledge may not be common, I have inserted a chapter on Vatican politics.

What did it matter that Ireland was on the rack of a law-imposed famine?* What did it matter that two millions of her people were dying† for want of the bread which they had produced from mother earth, but of which they had been robbed by landlordism—the cruel creature of English law? What did it matter that extermination by famine was the declared purpose of the government press,‡ and of government representatives, ‖ with respect to the Irish question? As a compensation for all this, it was surely sufficient that the church (which meant, and still means, the Italian Ring *in the church*) had made a great advance. The political ambition of three centuries had been attained! Glory hallelujah! the Pope's legate was again permitted to strut in the Court of St. James!

Joy reigned in Rome! Gloom spread over the camp of the Irish patriots!

"Their tents were all silent, their banners alone,
Their lances unlifted, their trumpets unblown."

---

* Irish famines are not NATURAL famines, they are ARTIFICIAL famines; they are not made by the Lord, but by the landlord; they are not famines of food—there is always plenty of that in Ireland—but famines of money with which to buy food from landlords, who have taken the fruits of the soil as rent for land, to which they have generally no moral title." Ireland of To-day, p. 184.

† Hist. of Our Own Times, Vol. I., p. 324.

‡ "In a few years," said the London Times, exultingly, "a Celtic Irishman will be as rare in Connemara as is the red Indian on the slopes of the Manhattan." Ireland Since the Union, p. 144.

‖ Ireland of To-day, pp. 46 and 191.

Right or wrong, for good or evil, another "Irish movement" lay dead at the feet of the triumphant Vatican!

The principal leaders of the movement were sentenced to be "hanged, disemboweled and quartered," but this barbarous sentence was commuted by Act of Parliament to transportation for life.* Of the others, numbers were convicted and hundreds fled to exile, and Ireland suffered not only the sacrifice of many of "her best and noblest sons," but also "in the terrible re-action, prostration, terrorism and disorganization that ensued."†

CHAPTER X.

THE FENIAN MOVEMENT OPPOSED BY THE CHURCH.

Passing over the Tenant League agitation, the next serious effort for the liberation of Ireland was the Fenian movement, organized by a few daring spirits in May, 1858.

The purpose was to organize and drill an Irish army; to have them supplied with munitions of war by similar organizations of Irishmen in America; to rise at a given signal; storm the English strongholds and proclaim Ireland free.‡ It was

---
* New Ireland. p. 125.
† New Ireland, p. 125.
‡ New Ireland, p. 264, et. seq.

too loosely organized, for a movement so serious, and was in many respects impracticable and reckless, but it was full of genuine patriotism, and love of a country whose condition was so wretched and desperate that it could not be seriously injured by their adventure.

Bishop Moriarty, of Kerry, within an hour after learning of the movement,* commenced a bitter warfare against it. The Catholic clergy were soon denouncing it throughout Ireland as a "secret society" unauthorized by the church.

Over this issue "the Fenian movement, on its very threshold, was plunged into a bitter war with the ecclesiastical authorities of the Catholic Church. 'The priest has no right to interfere in or dictate our politics,' said the Fenian leaders; 'ours is a political movement; they must not question us or impede us.' 'You cannot be admitted to the sacrament until you give up and repent of illicit oaths,' responded the Catholic priests, 'and if you contumaciously continue in membership of an oath-bound secret society, you are liable to excommunication.'"

"Do you hear this? We are cursed by the church for loving our country!" exclaimed the Fenians;" and thus the quarrel continued for five

---

* New Ireland, p, 264.

years.* The movement grew, and attained considerable proportions, but in face of such opposition it could not accomplish much.

In 1867 three of its promoters—Allen, O'Brien and Larkin—were hanged. These men died with the prayer: "God Save Ireland," on their lips; while their gentle Christian antagonist, Bishop Moriarty, of "unimpeachable loyalty"† regretted that "hell was not hot enough nor eternity long enough to punish such miscreants."‡

CHAPTER XI.

HOME RULE MOVEMENT OPPOSED BY THE CHURCH.

On the 19th day of May, 1870, the present Home Rule Movement was instituted. It was a purely peaceable movement to secure, by constitutional agitation, "the establishment of an Irish parliament, with full control over domestic affairs."‖ At this meeting were "men who never before met in politics save as irreconcilable foes. The Orangeman and the Ultramontane, the staunch Conservative and the sturdy Liberal, the National Repealer and the Imperial Unionist, the

---

* New Ireland, p. 312.
† See page 28.
‡ Parnell movement, p. 227.
‖ New Ireland, p. 450.

Fenian Sympathizer and the devoted loyalist, sat in free and friendly counsel."*

Even at this heterogeneous meeting the resolution in favor of Home Rule was adopted unanimously.

But the Catholic Bishop of Derry was more loyal to English rule than all of these, so he opposed the movement, and in January, 1871, he publicly denounced it.

Like Cardinal Cullen he "was always on the side of the Government as against all struggles of Nationalists, on the principle that England could do more for the interests of the church than any National Party."†

The British Government was at that time holding out a proposition to establish a Catholic University in Ireland, for the purpose of drawing the Catholic clergy away from the popular movement, and it had "a powerful effect with some of the Catholic bishops and clergy."‡ Early in 1872 the Home Rulers noticed that important newspapers under the control and influence of the Catholic clergy "began to draw off from the movement and to say that the demand for Home Rule was,

---
* New Ireland, p. 444.
† Parnell Movement, p. 140.
‡ New Ireland, p. 456.

no doubt, very right and just, but it was *inopportune.*"*

Did the finger of Rome direct this change of heart on the part of the Irish clergy? I cannot prove it by direct evidence, but viewing and judging the circumstances in the light of experiences prior and subsequent to that time, I may fairly say that it so appears to a moral certainty and beyond all reasonable doubt.

The movement grew and prospered, but the opposition of the clergy continued. On the 6th of August, 1875, at a banquet given in honor of the centenary of the birth of Daniel O'Connell, a number of Catholic clergymen, native and foreign, were present, and an unseemly discussion arose between the clergymen and the Home Rulers on the question of Home Rule, which resulted in much dissension, and, immediately afterwards, Mr. McSwiney, Lord Mayor of Dublin, organized, or tried to organize, a sort of clerical counter movement to draw away the strength of the Home Rule Party, calling it the "Faith and Fatherland Party."

On the 15th of August, 1879, the price of this clerical opposition to the Home Rule movement was duly paid by Parliament, by the abolition of

---

* New Ireland, p. 456.

the Queen's University in Ireland and the establishment in its stead of a new University for Roman Catholics.

CHAPTER XII.

THE LAND LEAGUE OPPOSED BY THE POPE.

In September, 1879, the Irish National Land League was formed, not to replace, but to supplement, the Home Rule movement.

Another artificial famine was approaching, and the real purpose of the League was to intercept landlord extortion and to check evictions; thus preventing the re-enactment of the horrible famine scenes of 1847-8.

The lives of many thousands of Irish families were saved, and this immediate success in giving shelter and protection to the masses of the people from the one ever dreaded enemy—landlordism—rallied the people in hundreds of thousands to the standard of Parnell and Davitt.

In the midst of this struggle to keep the unfortunate tenantry under the shelter of their own cabins during the famine; while subscriptions to the famine fund, for the relief of the starving Irish, were slowly arriving from the generous hearted of Canada, Australia, the United States, and even from far-off India ; and while factors and bailiffs and soldiers and constables and crowbar brigades were evicting the unfortunates and leveling their huts, and as far and fast as the passive resistance of the unarmed people would permit, re-enacting the horrors of 1847-8—even in this awful crisis—the Roman Catholic Archbishop of Dublin (McCabe), in full cry with the bloodhounds of landlordism, had a pastoral letter published in the churches of his arch-diocese condemning the Land League agitation.

On the 10th of October, 1880, and again on the 30th of October, 1881, the same Archbishop renewed his thunders against those who by passive resistance defended the lives and homes of the people, in new, and truly "loyal," pastoral letters. In March, 1881, a Ladies' Land League was formed for the most humane and Christian purpose of "raising funds, inquiring into cases of eviction, and affording relief to evicted tenants. As soon as this new organization came into existence it was assailed" by this red-cap-hunting hound of the Vatican—Archbishop McCabe—"as at once immodest and wicked."* As a reward for these services, and as an acknowledgment that he was sufficiently anti-Irish and cold-blooded to associate

---

* Ireland since the Union, p. 274.

in close relationship with the Italian Ring, he was created a cardinal* on the 27th of March, 1882.

I have spoken specially of the conduct of Archbishop McCabe because his elevation to the position of a "prince of the church" is pretty conclusive evidence that he, at least, in all that he did, was acting under the direct orders of the Vatican.

A strong circumstance tending to confirm this view is, that the Vatican, while still pretending to be neutral in the affairs of Ireland, was secretly interfering with the raising of funds in America, even to relieve the famine sufferers whose support had been undertaken by the Leagues.

In 1882, Rev. Edward McGlynn, the most eloquent and popular Catholic priest in the world, was delivering lectures in New York for the benefit of the Leagues. Archbishop McCloskey received peremptory orders from the Vatican requiring him to compel Dr. McGlynn to desist, on pain of suspension from his priestly office.

The Dr., bowing to authority, discontinued his lectures.

In 1883, Dr. McGlynn was requested to deliver a special lecture for the benefit of the then starving people of Western Ireland. A telegram was immediately sent to Archbishop McCloskey from

---

* He was the second Irish cardinal ever appointed; Cullen, another anti-Irish Irishman, being the first.

the Vatican, signed by Cardinal Simeoni, ordering him to "suspend this priest McGlynn, for preaching in favor of the Irish revolution."

These documents came to light in December, 1886, in consequence of the trouble between Dr. McGlynn and Archbishop Corrigan at that time. Otherwise the circumstances would never have been made public. How many hundred similar blows may have been dealt against the Irish cause in secret and in darkness by these Italian allies of England may never be known.

Another circumstance pregnant of meaning is, that, about the time of which I am speaking, it was reported that Sir George Errington, a "Castle Cawtholic," and emissary of England, was commissioned for some secret intrigue at the Vatican.

Michael Davitt went to Rome, as the accredited representative of the Irish people, to lay their cause before the Pope.

He was spurned and boycotted, as if he was a leper, by the "distinguished Catholics" then visiting at Rome—even the guests at the hotel where he stopped left the dining-room in which he was seated, and threatened to leave the hotel unless *he* was required to leave. He was refused an audience with the Pope, on the ground that his reception might give the impression that the Holy Father was taking sides on the Irish question.

A few weeks afterwards, the Prince of Wales, apparently for no other purpose than to expose the double face of the Vatican, had a suggestion conveyed to the Holy Office that *he* thought of paying a visit to Rome, and inquiring if he might expect to be accorded an audience by His Holiness.

Immediately, without any fear of misconstruction, the arms of the Holy Father were opened and extended to receive the representative of the *English* side of the Irish question. He did not go, but sent his "Castle Cawtholic" flunky, Errington, who was accorded more than one audience* and on his *ex parte* representations secured at least one important favor of which I shall presently speak.

On the 20th of January, 1883, Pope Leo XIII. sent a rescript to the Irish clergy commanding them to use their power to suppress certain classes of societies, the description being broad enough to include the Irish political leagues.

The effect of this rescript was not to destroy, as designed, but to divide and weaken the movement; but it certainly was not the Pope's fault if anything

---

* No representative of landlordism was ever denied an audience by the Pope.

remained of the Irish movement after his poisoned draught had been administered.

Not satisfied with this the Pope, on the 11th of May of the same year, issued a more powerful and mandatory rescript, condemning and forbidding disaffection to the government, and forbidding subscriptions to the Parnell testimonial fund, a fund then being raised by Irishmen and their sympathizers to reimburse Mr. Parnell for losses suffered by him through the agitation. This was the papal favor secretly granted at the secret request of Errington, made under circumstances which I have already detailed.

Again, upon the death of Cardinal McCabe in February, 1885, this same Errington, still "acting as the gutter-agent of the English Government," secretly secured from the Pope a rescript or order commanding the bishops of Ireland to observe the wishes of England in nominating a successor to the vacant archbishopric.

Before this rescript had reached Ireland, Errington, either in the intoxication of joy produced by the success of his mission, or under the influence of another kind of intoxication, quite common to his class of reveling Christians, boasted of the promise which he had secured from the Pope.

This news, telegraphed to Ireland before the

rescript had been received, called forth such a storm of indignation that the Pope, in fear of losing his Irish "Peter's Pence," recalled it.

In April, 1885, Bishop Nulty of Meath, a brave and noble patriot prelate, and others of his stripe, having publicly favored the Land League and Home Rule movements, were summoned to Rome and rebuked by the Pope for their disloyalty.

On the 9th of May following, Bishop Nulty published a pastoral letter warning the Vatican that if it persisted in its unjust and oppressive course toward the Irish people they too would some day manifest the spirit displayed by other nationalities and break away from the spiritual, as well as the temporal dominion of Rome. This pastoral is said to have "caused great *displeasure*." It did in fact cause great *consternation*, and produced the remarkable effect of keeping the Pope's hand away from the throat of Irish liberty for three full years.

CHAPTER XIII.

THE LAST RESCRIPT.

On the 20th of April, 1888, the Pope, at the secret and *ex parte* request of the Duke of Norfolk, issued another *rescript** condemning and forbidding the use of two of the weapons of self-defense invented and successfully used by the suffering people in their terrible and unequal struggle against the life-destroying oppression of landlordism, namely : the plan of campaign and the boycott.

This condemnation is put upon the grounds: (*a*) that the plan of campaign is " unjust and inequitable to the landlords; and (*b*) that the boycott is *"a new form of persecution* and proscription, altogether foreign to natural justice and to Christian charity."

Leaving out of account for the present the undenied and undeniable fact that the Irish landlords, under the protection of English laws, and English or pro-English judges, constables, bailiffs and soldiers, have been able, not only to hold their own, but to rob the whole Irish people of all the produce of their labor above that bare subsistence

---
* See Appendix C.

which is the portion of chattel slaves—denying even that to millions, whom they have willfully condemned to death by the slow tortures of famine—and to drive (as they still do) a million a decade into exile, let us consider what the plan of campaign and boycott are and compare them with the *methods* of persecution, plunder, and extermination which they were designed to resist.

CHAPTER XIV.

PLAN OF CAMPAIGN AND BOYCOTT *vs.* RACK RENT, EVICTION, AND RULES OF ESTATE.

The land question is at the very root, and is the root, of all the Irish troubles. The Irish people must live on the land, and from the land of Ireland, if they are permitted to live at all. There are now about five millions of people living on the Island, and the entire land on which and from which they must live is the exclusive private property of about seventeen thousand landlords, * great and small, who have the almost absolute power to determine upon what conditions and for what tribute the other millions shall be permitted to live. Having this power, the landlords, for

---

* Mullhall's Dictionary of Statistics, p. 266.

centuries, kept the people in a constant nightmare, and turned the country into a vast panorama of horrors.

They fixed rents according to the measure of their own merciless avarice, often making it higher than the gross yield of the land, and, in the language of Dean Swift, "*squeezed it out of the very blood and vitals and clothes and dwellings of the tenants, who live worse than English beggars.*" Whatever of the rent could not be extorted by the terrors of threatened eviction was generously allowed to accumulate in "arrearages," to pay which unusually good crops, and contributions of American relatives, were confiscated.

This is what, in Irelend, is called "rack-renting." It may be denominated the "rack" of landlordism, but it is not without its flesh-rending "spiked roller" (to use terms certainly familiar to the Holy Office of the Inquisition) nor its "fire wheel" and "torturing stake."

The tenant in arrears was always subjected to summary eviction, and even if his rent were not in arrears he was subject, on short notice, to be similarly evicted, in order that the owner might consolidate farms, or turn the land into a park, or sheep pasture, or in order to gratify any whim, revenge, or other desire, on the part of the landlord.

"Our Irish landlords," says Father Lavelle, "all Christians, *many of my own creed*,* act the landlord as if there were no God; oppressing the poor man and the weak of heart to put him to death."†

A parliamentary committee appointed to inquire into the condition of Irish tenantry—evicted in order to promote the consolidation of farms, *not for non-payment of rent*—reported that: "It would be impossible for language to convey an idea of the distress to which they have been reduced. * * * They are obliged to resort to theft and all manner of vice and iniquity to procure subsistence, and a vast number of them perish of want, after having undergone misery and suffering such as no language can describe and of which no conception can be formed without actually beholding it."‡

But the scope of this book will not permit the presentation of many examples of the murderous persecution by which landlordism has turned the heaven-favored land of Erin into the dark and

---

* Has the Pope ever excommunicated, or threatened to excommunicate, any of these landlords for persecuting their fellow Catholics? Not one.

† The Irish Landlord, p. 196.

‡ The Irish Landlord, p. 248.

bloody arena which it has certainly been. I have before me Father Lavelle's great and fascinating work on "The Irish Landlord," containing five hundred and forty pages filled with terrible but well attested examples of landlord atrocity, but those which I have, here and elsewhere in this volume given, are quite sufficient to show how unnatural is the power, and how terrible is the threat, of eviction. They show the sort of knife which the seventeen thousand landlords, in good and bad seasons, hold, by legal process, to the throats of their five million Irish tenant slaves,* to enforce their extortionate demands.

Well has Mr. Gladstone called the writ of eviction a "death warrant?"

But the landlord's persecution does not end with eviction. After eviction the unfortunate tenant must face the terrible "Rules of the Estate."

These rules forbid any tenant in the district giving food or shelter to any member of an evicted family, on pain of being in like manner evicted by *his* or *her* landlord. But this is not all, the landlords of other districts have equally stringent

---

* Pope Leo complimented the Emperor of Brazil on having freed his slaves, in the very week during which he ordered the Irish back into their chains.

rules against sheltering or harboring the doomed wretches.

Another example from Father Lavelle will illustrate the working of these rules. Speaking of a very ordinary eviction he says: "A certain landlord in County Galway got a cheap decree at quarter sessions against a tenant on his property. This was early in October; October and November passed over and a gleam of hope began to enter the poor man's soul that, at least, he would be permitted to pass the Christmas holidays in his old home. December was fast running out; the sun of Christmas eve had actually risen, and with it the poor man and his wife and family, when horror of horrors! what does he see approaching his cabin door, followed by a *posse comitatus* of the Crow-bar Brigade, but the Sheriff, surrounded by a detachment of the constabulary force. The family were flung out like vermin, and the work of demolition occupied but a few minutes. The evicted family passed that and the subsequent Christmas night with no other covering but that of the wide canopy of Heaven, as strict prohibitions had been issued to all the other tenants to harbor them on pain of similar treatment."*

Bishop Nulty of Meath, one of God's true

---

* The Irish Landlord, pp. 271-2.

noblemen, speaking of "a cruel and inhuman eviction" witnessed by himself, and in which "seven hundred human beings were driven from their homes in one day and set adrift on the world," although "there was not a single shilling of rent due on the estate at the time except by one man." After describing the horrors of the eviction itself, he proceeds: "The horrid scenes I then witnessed I must remember all my life long. The wailing of women—the screams, the terror, the consternation of children—the speechless agony of honest industrious men—wrung tears of grief from all who saw them. * * * The heavy rains that usually attend the autumnal equinoxes descended in cold, copious torrents throughout the night, and at once revealed to the houseless sufferers the awful realities of their condition. I visited them next morning and rode from place to place administering to them all the comfort and consolation I could. The appearance of men, women and children, as they emerged from the ruins of their former homes—saturated with rain, blackened and besmeared with soot, shivering in every member from cold and misery—presented positively the most appalling spectacle I ever looked at. The landed proprietors in a circle all around—and for many miles in every direction—warned their tenantry, with threats of their direst vengeance against the humanity of extending to any of them the hospitality of a single night's shelter. Many of these poor people were unable to emigrate with their families, while at home the hand of every man was thus raised against them. They were driven from the land on which Providence had placed them, and, in the state of society surrounding them, every other walk of life was rigidly closed against them. What was the result? After battling in vain with privation and pestilence, they at last graduated from the workhouse to the tomb, and in a little more than three years, nearly a fourth of them lay quietly in their graves."*

This is landlordism, in all its cold and cruel infamy! Standing between God's children and the means which he has provided freely for their support!† Blasting their happiness and crushing out their lives. Down with it! Eternal Justice, let it, and its supporters, find:

> "No shelter from the withering curse
> Of God and human kind."

But what of the plan of campaign and the boycott—the weapons of passive resistance

---

* The Parnell Movement, p. 173.
† It is estimated that Ireland, if free from landlordism, is capable of supporting comfortably from three to four times its present population.

with which the tenants, "contrary to natural justice and Christian charity" according to the Holy Father, seek to defend their lives and their families against this man-eating monster of landlordism?

The plan of campaign is a modification of the "No-Rent Manifesto" of October 18th, 1881, and is simply this: The tenants of a district determine to act together in withholding from their landlords enough of their crops, or of the price thereof, to provide food for their families and seed for their land for the approaching season, and to give the rest up to the landlord as toll for the privilege of using the God-given land. The tenants, or their representatives, agree upon the percentage of the fixed rents that can be paid by them, and then, all who desire to join in the plan, pay the amount of rent agreed upon to a secret agent (from whom it would be taken by legal process by the landlords if his identity were known), subject to future agreement between the landlord and tenants. If the landlord agrees to accept the rent thus deposited, it is paid over to him; otherwise it is returned to the tenant. The tenants, thus acting under the plan, assist each other in the defense of eviction suits, and, in defiance of the "Rules of Estate," give each other shelter when evicted.

But this would be ineffectual without some means of preventing their more unscrupulous fellow wretches from underbidding them and taking their little holdings at the old rack-rent rates.

Here the boycott comes into play, and it is simply this: Any person who rents the holding of an evicted tenant is socially, commercially, politically, and industrially ostracised by all of the other tenants (practically the whole population) in the district.

They will not associate with him, nor speak to him, nor buy from him, nor sell to him, nor work for him, nor hire him. They will not handle his grain, nor work where it is handled.

No member of any of the Leagues will work on any steamer which carries cattle raised by him to the English market. There is in it no invasion of legal right, and no aggression.

"Nothing is done *to* the obnoxious individual, but nothing will be done *for* him."*

This principle, as far as possible, is applied to obnoxious landlords as well as to underbidding tenants.

Thus the boycott and the plan of campaign are the complement and supplement of each other,

---

* Ireland Since the Union, p. 251.

and together they constitute a tolerably effective moral weapon of self-defense.

With the weapons which I have thus described the contest between landlordism and tenantry has of late years been fought.

This is the contest in which Pope Leo has deemed it his duty to interfere seven times, at least, within the past six years, and always on the side of the strong against the weak.

He now deems it his duty to disarm the unfortunate tenantry of even these moral weapons, and leave them naked and helpless to the cruel fangs of their worse than tiger enemies.

Vicar of Christ! Well,—so be it.

These condemned methods have saved thousands of the Irish people from starvation, and millions from hunger and privation, during the past six years.

They have saved to the people about fifteen millions of dollars per annum, and have, by this immediate benefit, consolidated the whole people of Ireland in the mighty political struggle for Home Rule and Land Reform.

The landlords, the Tories, and the Pope well know that, if this advantage could be taken away, the political movement would disintegrate with it; and so, by an agreement confessedly made with the Duke of Norfolk, the Pope threatens the Irish tenants with the terrors of an eternity in hell, after death, unless they will consent to return again to the hell on earth from which the Land and National Leagues have partially relieved them.

Before the condemned methods were adopted, from one million to five million dollars were annually sent to the people of Ireland by relatives and sympathizers in America, but the contributions served only to increase the rapacity and extortion of the landlords, by increasing the tenants' ability to pay—the only standard by which the *maximum* of Irish rents is measured. Any man, not an idiot, who speaks seriously of freedom of contract between landlords and tenants in Ireland, betrays a contemptible hypocrisy that not even the mask of the Gorgon would conceal.

If, by any possibility, the Pope may have been ignorant of the true nature of the controversy in which he has been so persistently interfering, his ignorance is due to his constant refusal to hear the Irish side of it, and is not a whit less excusable than malice *prepense*.

The other hypocritical defense so often urged, that the Pope does not oppose the Irish political *movement* but only *the methods* by which it is supported, is puerile and childish. The methods constitute the force and measure of the movement.

They alone make the political movement possible by giving the people an immediate incentive to combined effort, and a breathing spell from the tortures of landlordism, during which they may work and think.

Suppose that Germany were to commence an invasion of France (eldest daughter of the church) and that the Pope should forbid the French people to use either powder or improved implements of war in resisting the invasion. and should then, with customary hypocrisy, say to the French people: "My dear children, I would not for the world interfere with your ambition to preserve the political freedom of your country. I object only to your *methods.*"

What would the French people say to this?

They would burn him in effigy, as they did his predecessor, Pius VI., in 1791, when he interfered, on behalf of the nobility, with their political aspirations.

The ultramontanes will hardly deny the analogy between the present case of Ireland and the supposed case of France on the ground that France has a nationality to preserve while Ireland has not, since Ireland had a nationality for thirty centuries and would probably have had it to this time were it not for the treachery of Pope Leo's predecessor—Adrian.

This Roman "explanation of the rescript" is so supremely ridiculous, that, if it had been given by a negro minstrel it would have produced roars of laughter and would have ranked as "a good hit."

CHAPTER XV.

POPE LEO'S BOYCOTT ON DR. M'GLYNN.

In the Pope's *rescript* we are favored with the information that boycotting is "a new form of persecution and proscription." In truth, however, it is but a mild form of excommunication, suggested by, and modeled after, the Roman Catholic practice of religious and civil ostracism, which, according to Catholic church authorities, has been practiced by the church ever since its organization; was recommended by Christ* himself and actually put in practice by St. Paul.†

We find also, that Solon (594 B. C.), recommended the "ostracism" by the people of persons whose presence was considered dangerous to the

---

* Matt., XVIII., 17.
† 1 Cor., V. 3; Catholic Dic., p. 327.

peace and well being of Athens; but that boycott included the harsher element of "exclusion from the city."

In cases of major excommunication, *non tolerati*, pronounced by the pope or by any bishop of the Catholic church, "the faithful are forbidden to hold either religious or civil communication"* with the excommunicated person.

I certainly cannot give a better definition of boycotting than to say that it is an agreement between two or more persons not "to hold either religious or civil communication" with a third person. Yet that is the very definition which Catholic authorities give of the universal practice of the church, and certainly the Holy Office does not mean to condemn a regular and frequent practice of the Catholic church as "contrary to Christian charity."

The Pope himself has now a boycott in full force against Dr. Edward McGlynn of the city of New York; a boycott which is, in its terms, infinitely more rigorous and terrible than any ever declared or enforced by any secular body in Ireland.

The church boycott delivers the victim immediately, and for eternity, over to the devil; † the

---
* Catholic Dic., p. 328.
† Catholic Dic., p. 327.

faithful are forbidden to hold either religious or civil communication with him; they cannot attend a meeting at which he is to deliver a lecture without incurring the penalty of excommunication * by contagion; and if a Catholic, however devout, even if he have received communion within a month, should suddenly die while attending a lecture delivered by an excommunicated person, he must be deprived of Christian burial. †

The body of a devout Catholic is now lying in a public vault in New York City, and, because he died suddenly at one of Dr. McGlynn's lectures on social questions, is denied Christian burial by the archbishop. In other words, this dead man's body is denied Christian burial because, in his lifetime, he did not take part in carrying out the Pope's boycott against Dr. McGlynn. A very common regard for the ordinary proprieties should have induced His Holiness to declare his own boycotts off before condemning the milder Irish boycotts as un-Christian.

It is no answer to this "deadly parallel" to say that the Irish boycotts, although milder, are in fact more strictly observed than his. It is certainly not his fault that anybody associates with or

---

* So declared by Bishop McQuade of Rochester, N. Y.

† So declared by Archbishop Corrigan, N. Y.

speaks to, or deals with, Dr. McGlynn, after he has given an order which requires them to avoid him.

Again, what is the penalty for violating the Pope's *rescript* against the un-Christian practice of boycotting ? Why, *the violators of the rescript will simply be boycotted by the Pope !*

It is fortunate, as has been fully explained, that this document was not issued by the Pope *ex cathedra*, but was issued on the fallible advice of the Holy Office of the Inquisition, over the deliberations of which the Pope presides in person,* and it is therefore possible to recall it if it shall prove to be erroneous.

If it effects its purpose without serious opposition, there will be no further action taken about it ; so, also, if it be quietly ignored ; but if it be strenuously resisted it will be found to be erroneous and withdrawn.

At any rate that is the fixed reputation of the Vatican in the matter of issuing political bulls against the children of the church, and there is no reason to suspect a change of policy at this time.

* Catholic Dic., p. 447.

CHAPTER XVI.

VATICAN POLITICS—THE ITALIAN RING.

To get any clear idea of the motives and purposes of the Vatican in dealing with the Irish question it is absolutely necessary to have a general knowledge of the character (religious and political) of the papal office, and of the personnel of its incumbents at various periods, and also a knowledge of the origin, character and personnel of the College of Cardinals.

There is a vast difference between the Catholic religion, the Catholic church and the Catholic hierarchy. The first consists of principles and articles of faith; the second is the organization by and through which these principles and articles are taught and inculcated, and the third is the body of priestly officers charged with administering the affairs of the church and promoting the religion.

The religion is unchangeable, no matter how much the interpretation of its principles and articles may vary. The organization, which includes discipline, ceremonies, etc., may be changed by the hierarchy as the ever-changing conditions of the world may require.

The hierarchy is constantly changing and is subject to all the defects that are incident to human folly, ambition and vice.

It is with this changeable human hierarchy, and with it alone, that I am dealing; and it is acknowledged, by all Catholic writers, to have been at various times, good and bad, weak and strong, covetous and generous, worldly and disinterested. I shall therefore speak freely, feeling that none can be reasonably offended, in his religious sensitiveness, by the statement of "truths, however painful,"* which do not concern the integrity of his religious principles.

The controlling power of the Catholic hierarchy consists of the Pope and a college of seventy Cardinals.†

The Pope appoints the Cardinals and the Cardinals elect the Pope. The whole church organization is therefore under the absolute and exclusive control of a self-perpetuating body of seventy-one men.

The tremendous power wielded by those seventy-one men, cannot be questioned by any person, or body of persons, in the church; and if their political as well as their religious edicts are obeyed by Catholics, it will at once be apparent that their

---
* See Lives of the Popes, by J. C. Earle, p. 6.
† Catholic Dic., p. 119.

support must be of incalculable value to political sovereigns, and that the temptation to corruption and worldly ambition is enormous.

It will further appear, at once, that if the College of Cardinals should ever fall into the hands of a few designing families it would be impossible to prevent them from creating or perpetuating a most exclusive aristocracy, as powerful and irresponsible as any that ever held sway upon earth.

These are the very things that have transpired in the See of Rome.

The College of Cardinals for over eight hundred years (ever since it was created) * has been composed almost exclusively of Italians, and these have been nearly all members of a little Italian nobility consisting of a very few families.

While the great teachers, preachers, bishops, and priests, representing more than nine-tenths of the Catholic world, have been practically excluded (being admitted only in a small and powerless minority), brothers, cousins, uncles, nephews, and even fathers and sons, of the little Italian nobility, have for generation after generation sat beside each other in the College of Cardinals.

To illustrate this, a few examples, from standard Catholic authorities, will suffice :

---

* Catholic Dic., p. 118.

ALL "NOBLEMEN." 103

The present Pope, John V. R. L. Pecci, is the son of Count Domenico, and has a brother in the College of Cardinals[1]; Pius IX., John M. M. Ferretti, was the son of Count Jerome Ferretti and Countess Catharine Solazzi[2]; Gregory XVI., Bartholemew Albert Cappellari, "was born at Belluno, in Lombardy, September 18th, 1795, of parents belonging to the nobles of the place[3];" Pius VIII., Francis X. Castiglioni, was "born (November 20th, 1761) of noble family[4]" and appointed as his secretary Cardinal Albini, of the house of Albini, "one of the most illustrious and noble in Italy, *boasting* even of imperial alliances[5];" Leo XII., Hannibal della Genga, "was the son of Count Hillary della Genga[6];" and Pius VII., Barnabas Chiaramonti, who was a relative of Pius VI,[7] derived "high nobility" from his father.[8] These constitute the last five Popes, and the statement which I have given illustrates how the papacy is confined, not merely to Italians, but to the old Italian political aristocracy.

But that is not all; four of the Popes—Leo X.,

---
1 M. F. Egan in "The Century," May, 1888.
2 Shea's Life of Pius IX., p. 11.
3 The Last Four Popes, by Cardinal Wiseman, p. 376.
4 The Last Four Popes, p. 323.
5 The Last Four Popes, p. 330.
6 The Last Four Popes, p. 195.
7 The Last Four Popes, p. 328-9.
8 The Last Four Popes, p. 37.

Clement VII., Pius IV., and Leo XI.—were immediate members of the Medici family[1]; three Popes—Innocent III., his nephew Gregory IX., and Innocent XIII.—were immediate members of the Conti family[2]; two of the Popes—Sixtus IV. and his nephew Julius II.—were immediate members of the Rovere family[3]; two of the Popes—Nicholas III. and Benedict XIII.—were immediate members of the Orsini family[4]; two of the Popes—Calixtus III. and his nephew Alexander VI.—were immediate members of the Borgia family.[5]

Cardinal Cæsar Borgia was a son of Pope Alexander VI.,[6] and sat as a member of the College of Cardinals,[7] over which his father presided.

These are but a few examples taken from the lives of popes who lived and reigned since the time of Adrian and Alexander, and during the time that the Irish people have been taking so large a share of their politics from Rome.

The power and prestige of the papacy have

---

[1] Earle's Lives of the Popes, pp. 366, 374, 393 and 412.
[2] Earle's Lives of the Popes, pp. 266, 279, and 436.
[3] Earle's Lives of the Popes, p. 360.
[4] Earle's Lives of the Popes, pp. 298 and 437.
[5] Earle's Lives of the Popes, pp. 343 and 356.
[6] There was nothing illicit in this. The Pope was a married layman. The cardinals are not bound to choose one of their own body; a layman, and even a married man may be lawfully elected." Catholic Dic., p. 679.
[7] Earle's Lives of the Popes, p. 356.

always excited the most consuming ambitions and burning jealousies among the *eligible* families.

Each family, and combinations of families, in turn, sought to gain control of the College of Cardinals.

An example of this is given in the life of Alexander VI., who, " *To satisfy his ambition and exalt the princes of his own family*, too often outraged the laws of justice. It was with such views that he sought the ruin of the houses of Colonna and Orsini."*

This Borgia family was originally from Spain, and Earle, with Hefele and others, speak of Alexander VI. as an exceptionally "unworthy pope." This is undoubtedly true, but it does not alter the fact that the papacy has been in the hands of a very wicked, ambitious and designing man, who was duly elected to the papal chair and filled it for nine years, and that if he had succeeded in doing what his more favored Italian predecessors did, the Borgia family, instead of being hunted from Italy by Pope Julius II., as they were, might still be in control of the Vatican, making political trades with England and issuing rescripts to Ireland ; for, if they had once secured the necessary majority of their own family in the college, no

---
* Earle's Lives of the Popes, p. 357 ; quoting Mariana, Lib. 26.

power in or out of the church could have di-s lodged them.

Besides, no candid historian will claim that Alexander VI. was any worse than his predecessors, Sergius III., John X., John XI., John XII., John XVI., or John XIX., the first three of whom were "elevated to the papal throne by the intrigues of the notorious Marozia,"* and the last of whom, with Benedict VIII., *tried to have the Holy See made a legal "inheritance in their family."*†

These, bear in mind, were not anti-popes, but duly elected and recognized popes of the church, although Sergius III. was, for some years, an anti-pope before being elected to the papal chair.‡

We had, recently, an illustration of the nepotism and family influence still prevailing at the Vatican, in that, while the Irish priesthood, representing more genuine Catholics than does the Italian priesthood, had not a single representative in the College of Cardinals, and while the Italians had more than a two-thirds majority of that college, two youthful offshoots of the effete Italian nobility were sent to Queen Victoria, also a temporal and spiritual sovereign (head of the Episcopal Church) with some sort of a trinket as a jubilee gift, and,

---

* Earle's Lives of the Popes, p. 187, 190-2.
† Earle's Lives of the Popes, p. 209.
‡ Earle's Lives of the Popes, pp. 185-7.

on its safe delivery, *to honor the Queen*, they were both created cardinals. This is also an illustration of the closer relation between the "nobilities" of England and Italy than exists between the Italans and their Irish co-religionists.

The political scheming which has been resorted to for the purpose of securing control of the Holy See was worthy of modern political bosses, and is very interesting.

The Pope, who for the first six hundred years after Christ, was recognized simply as the Bishop of Rome; and exercised no jurisdiction beyond that See, was, until the year 1059 "chosen like other bishops by the clergy and people, with the assent of the neighboring bishops."*

In that year (1059) the College of Cardinals was instituted and consisted of six bishops.† The number of cardinals was gradually increased by succeeding popes, very much as our United States Supreme Court has been increased, and, no doubt, for the same purpose, namely: to change from time to time the balance of power. This practice continued for over five hundred years, when, in 1586, the number was finally fixed at not exceeding seventy.‡

---

* Catholic Dic., p. 678.
† Catholic Dic., 118, 679.
‡ Catholic Dic., 119.

The Holy See, as thus constituted, claims the Divine right to exercise political as well as religious sovereignty in every country. This claim was emphasized by Monsignor Preston, Vicar General of the Arch-diocese of New York, in his " New Year's Sermon" (January, 1888) in which he said: "Whoever says, I will take my religion from Rome but not my politics, *is not a good Catholic.*"

But it needed not the assurance of Monsignor Preston to advise us of the Pope's claim of temporal authority over his religious followers.

Prior to the year 860 the Pope was inducted into office as "Vicar of our Savior Jesus Christ," and the miter was placed upon his head as one of the emblems of his priestly authority.

Some time between the years 858 and 867, Pope Nicholas I. united a kingly crown with the miter, and between that time and the year 1200 (the exact date is uncertain), a second crown was added,[*] and the third crown was added about the year 1370, thus completing the tiara.

Ever since that time, "The tiara is placed on the Pope's head, *at his coronation*, by the second Cardinal Deacon, in the loggia of St. Peter's, with the words, ' Receive the tiara adorned with three

---

Catholic Dic., p. 795

crowns, and know that thou art Father of Princes and Kings, Ruler of the World, Vicar of our Savior Jesus Christ '."*

Even in this coronation ceremony, as in the practice of the Vatican, the religious office is subordinated to the political offices.

In face of all these undenied and undeniable facts, how silly it is to enter into nice disputations about the religious character of the Pope's *rescript*.

The *rescript* was issued by the Pope as a temporal sovereign, was intended as a political edict, and obedience to it will be an acknowledgment that the self-revolving, self-perpetuating Italian Ring which I have described, has a Divine right to rule in the political affairs of Ireland.

It can have no other meaning.

---

* Catholic Dic., p. 796, citing "Beitrage," by Bishop Hefele, Vol. II., p. 236, et. seq.

CHAPTER XVII.

CONCLUSION.

The true and manly position of the Irish people in this matter must be, that, whatever its purpose, the *rescript* is an impudent interference with Irish politics and ought to be promptly and effectually repudiated.

It will not do to change the movement in order to avoid the letter, or meet the spirit, of the rescript, for that will instantly destroy the confidence of sympathizers everywhere.

Well may such sympathizers ask, as many even now are asking: What is the use of helping Irish movements if the Pope can still kill them, as for seven hundred years he has been killing them, just at the critical moment of dawning victory?

A quietus must now and forever be put upon Irish political rescripts from Rome. Otherwise confidence in " Irish movements " will be, for another generation, absolutely destroyed.

The spirit displayed by so many thousands of the Irish people, both in Ireland and America, in their protests against this latest edict, is most gratifying and encouraging; but there have also been manifested some of the old and fatal symptoms of disintegration, which have always been observed to follow papal rescripts. For example, at the meeting held in Limerick on Sunday, May 27th, while twenty thousand enthusiastic people, in spite of the bishop's anathemas, attended, it was observed that "there were no priests present, and the leading Catholics, who had previously been conspicuous *at* the meetings, were to-day conspicuous by their absence."

The meaning of this is too plain to students of Irish history.

It means, unless checked by prompt and effective measures, disintegration and death to the Irish Home Rule movement.

Are there no patriotic priests in Limerick? Yes, but true to the prophecies of Burke and Pitt and Sheil, Maynooth and Rome have established in them a principle of subserviency stronger than their patriotism—a readiness to sacrifice the interests of Ireland and the hopes and aspirations of her people to the discipline imposed by the church authorities at Rome.

In this crisis and in the future political struggles it is manifest that one of two things must be done: the Irish priests must break away from their slavish subserviency to the Italian Ring and reassume the independent position which was held by the clergy of Ireland from the time of St. Patrick to the coming of Cardinal Paparo; or if that, unfortunately, cannot be, then the people must break away from all political alliance with the priesthood and absolutely reject it as an element in political affairs; or finally, failing both of these, the Irish people must be content to wear the chain of England with the chain of Rome, until some future generation shall discard both chains together.

It is not necessary that any change should be made, either by priest or people, in their religion.

There were Irish saints, afterwards canonized by the Roman Church, who never recognized any allegiance to the See of Rome, except to receive the abstract doctrines of Catholicity from that centre; but I venture, on the authority of their canonization, to say, that they were at least as good Catholics as any of the ultramontane Irishmen of the present day.

Neither is it necessary that there should be any change in their relations to the church as an organization, but only that the Roman hierarchy be held strictly to their spiritual trust and boycotted, if necessary, out of their political pretensions.

If the people of Ireland would, by general concert of action, suspend payments on the bill of sale of Ireland, given by Pope Adrian to King Henry II., until the liberty which that instrument blasted shall be recovered, nothing more would be heard forever of papal interference with Irish politics, and the Irish priests would be left free to hasten the renewal of tribute.

LIST OF AUTHORITIES.

Of the many of the authorities which I have cited, there are several editions differently paged. To avoid misleading and hyper-criticism, I here insert a list of my authorities with the edition referred to:

TITLE.	EDITION.	AUTHOR.
History of Ireland	Kelly, 1885	M. Haverty
History of Ireland	Virtue, E. & R., 1845	S. O'Halloran
History of Ireland	First	Thos. Wright
History of Ireland	2nd O'Kelly's Trans.	Abbe MacGeoghegan
History of Ireland	Cameron & F.	D'Arcy McGee
History of Ireland	Kenmare Convent, 1876	M. F. Cusack
History of Ireland	Donahoe, 1857	Thos. Mooney
History of Ireland	Virtue, E. & R., 1845	Wm. Dolby
History of Ireland	Cameron & F.	John Mitchell
Irish before the Conquest	First	M. C. Ferguson
Irish Hierarchy	Sadlier, 1855	Rev. Thos. Walsh
Ecclesiastical Hist. of Ireland	Cummisky, 1838	Rev. P. J. Carew
Irish Landlord, The	Donahoe, 1870	Rev. P. Lavelle
Ireland As She Is	Kelly, 1877	J. J. Clancy
Ireland of To-day	Bancroft, 1881	M. F. Sullivan
New Ireland	Third	A. M. Sullivan
History of Our Own Times	Belford, C. & Co., 1887	Justin McCarthy
Outlines of Irish History	First	Justin McCarthy
Ireland Since the Union	Belford, C. & Co., 1887	Justin McCarthy
Lights and Shades of Ireland	French, 1851	Mrs. A. Nicholson
The Parnell Movement	Benziger, 1886	T. P. O'Connor
Catholic Dictionary	Catholic Pub. Society, 1884	Addis & Arnold
The Last Four Popes	Donahoe, 1858	Cardinal Wiseman
Life of Pius IX.	Kelly, 1877	J. G. Shea
Lives of the Popes	Kelly, 1877	J. C. Earle
The Pope	Pustet, 1885	Monsignor Capel
English Misrule	Lynch, C. & M., 1877	Rev. T. N. Burke

APPENDIX A.

Full translation of the Bull of Pope Adrian IV., granting Ireland to King Henry II.

[From O'Halloran's History of Ireland, p. 305.]

"Adrian, bishop, servant of the servants of God, to his dearest son in Christ, the illustrious King of England, greeting, and apostolical benediction:

"Full laudably and profitably hath your magnificence conceived the design of propagating your glorious renown on earth, and completing your reward of eternal happiness in heaven; while as a Catholic prince, you are intent on enlarging the borders of the church, teaching the truth of the Christian faith to the ignorant and rude, extirpating the roots of vice from the field of the Lord, and for the more convenient execution of this purpose, requiring the counsel and favor of the apostolic See, in which the maturer your deliberation and the greater the discretion of your procedure, by so much the happier we trust will be your progress, with the assistance of the Lord, as all things are used to come to a prosperous end and issue, which take their beginning from the ardor of faith and the love of religion.

"There is, indeed, no doubt but that Ireland, and all the islands on which Christ, the sun of righteousness hath shone, and which have received the doctrine of the Christian faith, do belong to the jurisdiction of St. Peter and the Holy Roman Church, as your excellency also doth acknowledge; and therefore, we are the more solicitous to propagate the righteous plantation of faith in this land, and the branch acceptable to God, as we have the secret conviction of conscience that this is more especially our bounden duty. You then, my dear son in Christ, have signified to us your desire to enter into the island of Ireland, in order to reduce the people to obedience under the laws, and to extirpate the plants of vice; and that you are willing to pay from each [house] a yearly pension of one penny to St. Peter, and that will preserve the rights of the churches of the land whole and inviolate. We, therefore, with that grace and acceptance suited to your pious and laudable design, and favorably assenting to your petition, do hold it good and acceptable, that, for extending the borders of the church, restraining the progress of vice, for the correction of manners, the planting of virtue, and the increase of religion, you enter this island, and execute therein whatever shall pertain to the honor of God and welfare of the land; and that the people of this land receive you honorably, and reverence you as their lord; the rights of their churches still remaining sacred and inviolate, and saving to St. Peter the annual pension of one penny from every house.

"If then you be resolved to carry the design you have conceived into effectual execution, study to form this nation to virtue and manners, and labor by yourself, and others you shall judge meet for this work, in faith, word, and life, that the church may be there adorned; that the religion of the Christian faith may be planted and grow up, and that all things pertaining to the honor of God, and salvation of souls, be so ordered, that you may be entitled to the fulness of heavenly reward from God, and obtain a glorious renown on earth throughout all ages. Given at Rome, in the year of Salvation 1156."

APPENDIX B.

Full translation of the Bull of Pope Alexander III., confirming the grant of Adrian.

[From O'Halloran's History of Ireland, page 306.]

"Alexander, bishop, servant of the servants of God, to his most dear son in Christ, the illustrious King of England, health and apostolical benediction.

"Forasmuch as these things, which have been on good reasons granted by our predecessors, deserve to be confirmed in the fullest manner, and considering the grant of the dominion of the realm of Ireland by the venerable Pope Adrian, we, pursuing his footsteps, do ratify and confirm the same, (reserving to St. Peter, and to the Holy Roman Church, as well in England as in Ireland, the yearly pension of one penny from every house) provided that the abominations of the land being removed, that barbarous people, Christians only in name, may, by your means, be reformed, and their lives and conversation mended, so that their disordered church being thus reduced to regular discipline, that nation may, with the name of Christians, be so in act and deed. Given at Rome, in the year of Salvation 1172."

APPENDIX C.

THE TEXT OF THE LAST RESCRIPT.

(From the "Dublin Freeman," May 5th, 1888.)

The following is a translation of the Latin text of the circular addressed by the Congregation of the Holy Office to the Irish Bishops in reference to the Plan of Campaign and to boycotting:—

MY LORD—A letter was issued by the Supreme Congregation of the Holy Roman and Universal Inquisition on the 20th of the present month of April, for transmission to the Archbishops and Bishops of Ireland.

Herewith I send your Lordship a copy of this letter, and having discharged this duty, and wishing you every blessing in the Lord, I remain yours devotedly,

JOHN CARDINAL SIMEONI, Prefect.

✠ D. ARCHBISHOP OF TYRE, Secretary.

S. Congregation of the Propaganda, Rome, April 23rd, 1888.

[COPY.]

MY LORD—Whenever the affairs of their country seemed to require it the Apostolic See has frequently addressed to the Irish people—towards whom it has always shown special affection—seasonable words of warning and counsel with the object of enabling them to defend or to assert their rights without prejudice to justice or to public tranquillity. At the present moment our Holy Father Pope Leo XIII., fearing lest right conceptions of justice and charity should be perverted amongst that people in consequence of that mode of warfare called the Plan of Campaign, which has been employed in that country in contests between letters and holders of lands or farms, as also in consequence of a form of proscription in connection with the same contests known as boycotting, commissioned the Supreme Congregation of the Holy Roman and Universal Inquisition to make the matter the subject of grave and careful examination. Accordingly the following question was submitted to the Most Eminent Fathers who share with me the office of General Inquisitors against heretical error, viz: In contests between letters and holders of lands or farms in Ireland is it lawful to have recourse to those means known as the Plan of Campaign and Boycotting—

and their Eminences, having long and maturely weighed the matter, replied in the negative.

Our Holy Father confirmed and approved this reply on Wednesday, the 18th of the present month.

How equitable this decision is any one will see who reflects that a rent fixed by mutual consent cannot, without violation of contract, be reduced at the arbitrary will of the tenant alone. This the more, since for the settling of such contests courts have been established which, allowance being made even for failure of crops or of disasters which may have occurred, reduce excessive rents and bring them within the limits of equity.

Again, it cannot be held to be lawful that rent should be extorted from tenants and deposited with unknown persons, no account being taken of the landlord.

Finally, it is altogether foreign to natural justice and to Christian charity that a new form of persecution and of proscription should ruthlessly be put in force against persons who are satisfied with, and are prepared to pay the rent agreed on with their landlord; or against persons who in the exercise of their right take vacant farms.

Your lordship will therefore—prudently but effectively—admonish the clergy and the people in reference to this matter, and exhort them to observe Christian charity, and not to overstep the bounds of justice whilst seeking relief from the evils which afflict them.—Your devoted servant in the Lord,   R. CARD. MONACO.

Rome, 20th April, 1888.

www.ingramcontent.com/pod-product-compliance
Lightning Source LLC
Chambersburg PA
CBHW020128170426
43199CB00009B/680